Scholar Bishop
The Recollections and Diary of Narcissus Marsh
1638–1696

IRISH NARRATIVES

IRISH NARRATIVES
Series edited by David Fitzpatrick

Personal narratives of past lives are essential for understanding any field of history. They provide unrivalled insight into the day-to-day consequences of political, social, economic or cultural relationships. Memoirs, diaries and personal letters, whether by public figures or obscure witnesses of historical events, will often captivate the general reader as well as engrossing the specialist. Yet the vast majority of such narratives are preserved only among the manuscripts or rarities in libraries and archives scattered over the globe. The aim of this series of brief yet scholarly editions is to make available a wide range of narratives concerning Ireland and the Irish over the last four centuries. All documents, or sets of documents, are edited and introduced by specialist scholars, who guide the reader through the world in which the text was created. The chosen texts are faithfully transcribed, the biographical and local background explored, and the documents set in historical context. This series will prove invaluable for university and school teachers, providing superb material for essays and textual analysis in class. Above all, it offers a novel opportunity for readers interested in Irish history to discover fresh and exciting sources of personal testimony

David Fitzpatrick teaches history at Trinity College, Dublin. His books include *Politics and Irish Life, 1913–1921* (1977, reissued 1998), *Oceans of Consolation: Personal Accounts of Irish Migration to Australia* (1995) and *The Two Irelands, 1912–1939* (1998).

For a full list of titles in the *Irish Narratives* series see inside front cover.

Scholar Bishop

The Recollections and Diary of Narcissus Marsh 1638–1696

Edited by

Raymond Gillespie

First published in 2003 by
Cork University Press
Crawford Business Park
Crosses Green
Cork
Ireland

Reprinted 2021

British Library Cataloguing in Publication Data
A CIP catalogue record for this book is available from the British Library.

A CIP record for this book is available from the Library of Congress.

ISBN 978 1 85918 338 0

Typesetting by Red Barn Publishing, Skeagh, Skibbereen, Co. Cork
Printed and bound by CPI Group (UK) Ltd, Croydon, CR0 4YY

www.corkuniversitypress.com

Contents

Acknowledgements

In 1701 Narcissus Marsh, Archbishop of Dublin, founded a library. Three hundred years later the library still survives and is still used by scholars, although their scholarship is of a different order to what Marsh would have recognised. This edition of the 'diary' of the founder of Marsh's Library was planned as part of the tercentenary celebrations of that library . Those who now run the library, Muriel McCarthy and Ann Simmons, have been immensely supportive of the project and have borne cheerfully the sometimes eccentric requests of the editor. Without their practical help, especially the computer skills of Ann Simmons, this edition would not have been possible. An intelligible rendering of Marsh's Latin and Greek was achieved only with the help of Jane Power, Angela Malthouse, Anthony Harvey and Michael Clarke. The introduction has been enhanced by references supplied by Toby Barnard to sources which I might otherwise have overlooked. I am grateful to the Governors and Guardians of Archbishop Marsh's Library and the Bodleian Library, Oxford for permission to reproduce texts. The enthusiasm of David Fitzpatrick, who saw the potential of the religious musings of a long-dead eccentric to instruct, and possibly even to entertain, has made this project a reality.

Introduction

On the evening of 20 December 1690 Narcissus Marsh, former Provost of Trinity College, Dublin, and since 1683 Bishop of Ferns and Leighlin, sat down to write a memoir of his life. Intermittently over the next seven days, between writing letters, attending to diocesan business, spending time in prayer and engaging in mathematical inquiry, he added to his narrative. By 27 December he had penned an account of his life and experiences, noting 'Lord make me often & seriously to reflect on what is past & prepare me for what is to come.'[1]

This sort of godly stocktaking of one's life was not an unusual occurrence in late seventeenth- and early eighteenth-century Ireland. Marsh's reforming colleague on the episcopal bench, William King, Bishop of Derry, wrote a similar survey of his life in 1703 when he was appointed Archbishop of Dublin.[2] There also exists a rather similar autobiographical narrative of a near contemporary of Marsh, the Rev. Devereux Spratt, Rector of Mitchelstown, County Cork, who died in 1688.[3] In this Spratt surveyed his life, recording both the providential acts of God towards him and also God's judgments on him which led to days of humiliation in repentance for his sins. The writing of these sorts of autobiographical works, which also served as quasi-spiritual narratives, was not the sole preserve of Church of Ireland clergymen. The Dublin Presbyterian minister the Rev. John Cook, on reaching the age of twenty-one in 1698, considered 'that (according to the custom of many pious and worthy Christians) it is high time to keep a more strict account of my life, together with the more remarkable transactions of my times especially as they regard myself'.[4] Like Marsh he penned a narrative of his life up to that point, and over the next twelve years he made occasional additions to his work recording important events in his life. Nor was this literary form confined to clergy. The Killyleagh Presbyterian merchant James Trail in the early eighteenth century constructed a very similar document in the blank pages of one of his account books, and like Marsh and Cook he continued to add entries to it throughout most of his life.[5]

Marsh's text stands firmly in the Irish Protestant tradition of the 'godly narrative'. Some were similar to it, but others were rather different. It has few similarities, for instance, with the sort of conversion narratives written by many of the godly seeking admission to gathered churches or voluntary associations. These were usually fairly stereotyped documents constructed around a drama which began with a sense of sin, often awakened by the preaching of a godly minister, a period of searching, and finally a conversion experience in which spectacular divine intervention, sometimes through dreams or celestial lights, was involved. If the author was unsure of the formulae, a godly minister was often on hand to guide his or her pen or to edit the resulting product so as to conform to an ideal model. John Rogers, the minister of the Independent church which met at Christ Church, Dublin in the 1650s, happily edited the fifty-five narratives of the lives he collected from his congregation to make them fit an approved model of the conversion story.[6] Marsh, however, worked within a rather different set of literary conventions. These were more cautious and rejected the sort of showy enthusiasm of conversion that characterised the dissenting conversion narrative, preferring to emphasise instead a more restrained and interiorised godly piety which blends into self-possession to produce a decent reticence about personal affairs.[7] Marsh's narrative was certainly never intended for public circulation as many conversion narratives were, and indeed fear that such a narrative might have had too wide a circulation may account for the fact that William King chose to compose his own reflections on his life in Latin.

Several factors may have operated together to encourage Marsh to begin his recollections in December 1690. The fact that it was his fifty-second birthday may betray a growing sense of his age, although he was to live another twenty-three years, which is slightly above the life expectancy of a male contemporary who had reached the age of fifty. The fact that he was unmarried and childless may also have been a contributory factor to his concern with ageing. Probably more unsettling were the events of the previous two years when, as a result of Catholic resurgence under James II, Marsh had been forced to flee to England in

March 1689, returning to Ireland only five months before he began his narrative. This upheaval clearly had a considerable psychological impact on Marsh, especially in the light of his fear of Catholicism as revealed in some of the dreams he recorded in his tract. Apart from this, he was parted from his books which had been left in the episcopal residence in Carlow. This was a considerable wrench for a man such as Marsh who was consumed by intellectual curiosity. As he commented in February 1693, ''tis now above four years y^{t} I have been deprived of the use of my books but I hope I shall shortly be restored to y^{m} and they to me'. When they were reunited, Marsh noted in his diary that he spent a long period 'in my studies'.[8]

Whatever the context which prompted Marsh to write, the immediate circumstance of his taking up his pen was the news which he heard on 19 December that he was to be elevated to the archbishopric of Cashel. Appointment to a senior ecclesiastical position would not have been unusual for someone of Marsh's background, and his appointment as Bishop of Ferns and Leighlin called for little comment in his narrative. Indeed, his predecessor and successor as Provost of Trinity College had both been elevated to bishoprics; and of the twenty men appointed to the Irish bench of bishops between 1691 and 1699, nine had been fellows of Trinity. Appointment to a metropolitan see was a rather different matter. The capacities of two of the other archbishops, Francis Marsh of Dublin and Primate Michael Boyle of Armagh, were impaired by age. Boyle was rapidly moving towards senility, and Francis Marsh died, to be replaced by Narcissus (to whom he was not related), in 1693. The appointment to Cashel established Marsh as one of the most senior ecclesiastical figures in Ireland and offered him a promising future. It was clearly time to take stock of his life.

As a result of this stocktaking of his life, Narcissus Marsh poured out onto paper what seemed to him the most significant events and experiences of his life. Part of the information he recorded, and subsequently added to, was straightforwardly biographical, and most of what is known of Marsh's early life consists of what is preserved in his narrative. He noted his birth in 1638 at Hanington in north-east Wiltshire in an area marked by its cultural and religious conservatism, reflected in its unwavering support for the king during the English Civil War of the 1640s.[9] Given this background, it is perhaps strange that Marsh should have elected to attend Magdalen Hall, an Oxford college with distinctly Puritan tendencies. Magdalen's influence is perhaps reflected in Marsh's austerity commented on by Archbishop King in his funeral sermon (Appendix 3 below) and his youthful custom of fasting during Lent recorded in the narrative. However, Marsh had certainly been exposed to such godly ideas earlier in his life, since one of those he names in his narrative as one of his schoolmasters, the Rev. John Crouch, was from this tradition. He was presented at the Wiltshire quarter-sessions in 1661 for refusing to use the Book of Common Prayer and became a separatist preacher in London.[10] This combination of conservatism, with its loyalty to the Established Church, and godly piety of the 1650s shaped Marsh's outlook profoundly. However, Magdalen Hall had another influence on Marsh. It inculcated into him an enthusiasm for scholarly endeavour, and since the college was one of the main centres in Oxford for the study of oriental languages, it is not surprising that Marsh remained passionately committed to this area of learning throughout his life and collected oriental manuscripts with enthusiasm.[11] His interest in mathematics, astronomy and oriental languages probably recommended him to Seth Ward, Bishop of Exeter and early member of the Royal Society, who was prepared to offer the recently ordained Marsh a chaplaincy. Marsh himself was reluctant to become a parish clergyman and only briefly held a living, that of Swindon near his birthplace. This was not due to lack of opportunity, since after the Restoration there was a shortage of suitable clergy, which may explain why Marsh was ordained before the canonical age. Rather, as Marsh himself claimed, his intellectual curiosity was greater than his enthusiasm for administration, and as a result he stayed at Oxford. By 1673 he had become principal of St Alban's Hall, where, according to the Oxford gossip Anthony Wood, 'by the good discipline that he kept up and maintained made it flourish more than it had done for many years before'.[12] He also acquired a powerful patron in John Fell, Dean of Christ Church, Oxford, and after 1675 Bishop of Oxford. As a senior member of the university, Fell was well known to its Chancellor, James Butler, Duke of Ormond, and this nexus was to be important in the course of Marsh's career.

The first fruit of the Fell–Ormond connection was Marsh's appointment as Provost of Trinity College, Dublin in 1678, following the promotion of Michael Ward to the bishopric of Ossory. Marsh is strangely silent about his period in Trinity, although it did produce a number of achievements which he recorded later in a letter of 1706 which is printed as Appendix 1 below. This records the considerable impact Marsh had on the institution, including his significant reforms in the running of the college library and his important role in the project to revise and publish Bishop Bedell's translation of the Old Testament into Irish.[13] Despite this activity, Marsh was certainly unhappy in Trinity. Throughout his life in Ireland he continued to feel himself isolated from the wider scholarly community, and he maintained a network of scholarly correspondents in Oxford to keep him informed of developments there. In 1698 he noted: 'I live out of the way of learning where I can have no account of what is going abroad in ye world but from England.'[14] Moreover, when he quoted the Bible in his narrative, it is usually from the Old Testament prophets in exile that he found an apposite text. Dublin was also a rapidly growing and at times a rather unpleasant city, or, as Marsh noted in his narrative, a 'lewd debauch'd town'. Marsh recorded that when trying to observe the comet over Dublin in 1681 he had difficulty in seeing it 'through ye smoke of ye town which many times rendered it invisible here when three miles off ye place it might be well seen'. What annoyed him most was the 'constant round of business', and this was what made the life of a rural bishop preferable to that of a society provost.[15] The further intervention of his patron, John Fell, secured him the see of Ossory in 1682, where, in the words of the narrative, 'I continued quiet in my B[isho]pric'.[16] That quietness was disturbed by the accession of James II to the throne. The Catholicisation policy of Lord Deputy Tyrconnell made life difficult for the senior Church of Ireland clergy. What that meant for Marsh is suggested by his account of one event at Ferns in 1688, printed as Appendix 2 below. This sort of petty harassment over the rights of the church, whether real or perceived, was too much for many of the Church of Ireland hierarchy, and most fled to England, where in March 1689 Marsh joined them.

Marsh's sojourn of over a year in England was to be of considerable importance for his later career. He became prominent among the Irish exile community in London and worked with John Vesey, Archbishop of Tuam, to acquire livings for exiled clergy.[17] More significantly, Marsh made contacts with a number of influential figures in the English church and at court, most of whom feature in his narrative as correspondents in England after his return to Ireland. Particularly important were Gilbert Burnet, Bishop of Salisbury, Henry Compton, Bishop of London, and William Lloyd, Bishop of St Asaph. Lloyd probably already knew of Marsh through his involvement in the plan to print the Irish translation of the Old Testament. Lloyd was consulted over the financing of the project because he had previously been involved in the publication by subscription of a Welsh translation of the Bible. Both men had similar views on the dangers of nonconformity and the need to promote a campaign for moral reformation to increase piety in both England and Ireland, and it was Lloyd who found Marsh a benefice that would provide an income during his exile. It was, however, Burnet who lobbied for a better position for Marsh in Ireland, and in December 1690, five months after his return from England, he was appointed to the archbishopric of Cashel.[18]

Marsh's appointment to Cashel was only the beginning of a rapid ascent of the offices of the church, and consequently those of the state. In 1694, on the death of Francis Marsh, he was elevated to the see of Dublin, the news of which 'laid me grovelling on the Ground in my Chamber at Cork for the Terror of it'.[19] After the death of the senile and blind Primate Boyle in December 1702 Marsh succeeded him as Archbishop of Armagh in the following month. Such a rise through the church hierarchy brought civil administrative duties and Marsh served a number of short periods as a Lord Justice in 1699, 1701–2, 1707–8 and 1710. Unfortunately after 1696 he failed to make any new additions to the narrative he had begun in December 1690, and since very few of his own letters survive, other contemporary narratives of his life, such as those printed in Appendices 3 and 4 below, need to be pressed into service to reconstruct his later years. William King, Archbishop of Dublin, drew attention to many of the characteristics of Marsh' s later life in the sermon preached at his funeral which is printed as Appendix 3. He highlighted Marsh's continuing interest in scholarship, which reflected itself in the collecting of manuscripts and books (culminating in the foundation of a public library at St Patrick's in 1701) rather than in publication, and also praised his piety and his concern to build up (sometimes literally) the Irish church. However King's rather eulogistic picture is counterbalanced by the account of Dean Swift (Appendix 4), who blamed Marsh for his own lack of advancement in the church, and painted a picture of a rather inept figure somewhat at odds with the world in which he lived.

The closing years of Marsh's life are a story of slow decline. He complained of a 'weakness in my right arm' in 1704, and he probably suffered a mild stroke in 1707 but seems to have made a fairly full recovery. By 1711 he was seriously ill, and had been so for some time, and his illness was impeding the work of Convocation.[20] Indeed, so poor was his condition that many people believed he was dying. In the event, he survived another two years and died on 2 November 1713 and was buried five days later in the graveyard of St Patrick's Cathedral.

Apart from straightforward biographical material, Marsh provided other sorts of information in his narrative. He recorded, almost accidentally, a great deal about his attitudes to the world in which he lived, and in particular he laid out his religious beliefs for inspection. All the contemporaries who commented on Marsh were unanimous in recording his deep spirituality. There is no reason to doubt that this was, as King claimed in his funeral sermon, anchored firmly in the Bible and the traditions of the Church of England, especially the Book of Common

Prayer. Indeed, in his narrative, when Marsh addressed his God in short prayers in the text, the language he used was not that which he deployed in writing his main narrative but rather that of the Authorised Version of Scripture or the Book of Common Prayer. However, Marsh's religious world extended outside this tradition. What held both Marsh's world and his narrative together was a sense that God's providence ordered men's affairs in the world. This was a common assumption in both England and Ireland in the seventeenth century; but how it was worked out, even within Protestantism, varied from group to group. The godly separatist tradition tended to see God's providence at work in the unusual, especially wonders in the natural world, which they interpreted in a highly personal way as a sign of God's special providence towards them. Marsh certainly had tendencies in this direction. One indication of this is the detail with which he records the dreams of his youth, to which he clearly attached considerable significance. While most orthodox Protestants regarded dreams as a purely natural phenomenon, Marsh was prepared to go further, declaring in his narrative that it was 'wonderfull that a man's reason should act so strongly when he is sleeping; unless we look upon such dreams to come from God as many of them do'.[21] While Marsh may have seen these dreams as revelations of a sort, he was uncomfortable with them and did not venture any personal interpretation as to what they might mean, although he was clearly unsettled by one dream which predicted his elevation to the episcopacy. He might travel some way along the spiritual road with the godly, but he preferred the communalism of the Anglican tradition rather than the individualism of the godly.

Such positive attitudes towards personal revelations to individuals were uncommon among orthodox divines by the end of the seventeenth century. The disruption of the 1650s, with its emphasis on personal interpretation of revelation, encouraged late seventeenth-century theologians in the Established Church, under the leadership of John Tillotson, Archbishop of Canterbury, whom Marsh had met in London in 1689, to urge a shift from the world of special providences towards the world of the ordinary. Understood from this perspective, the entire world was a revelation of God. As Marsh himself noted in his journal for 26 April 1693, 'O Lord grant that in studying thy works we may also study to promote thy Glory (which is the true end of all our studies) & prosper O Lord our understanding for thy name's sake.'[22] It is in this context that Marsh's passion for study, and particularly the study of mathematics, needs to be understood. For Marsh the study of mathematics and the natural world was not simply an intriguing puzzle but a religious duty. For him science and religion were part of a seamless whole. As his diary entries for 26 December 1690 or 7 January or 18 May 1691 reveal, the solution of a mathematical problem was also an occasion for prayer and religious rejoicing, since to him such a solution reflected the truth of God.

There can be little doubt of the power of such a spirituality based on a providential understanding of the actions of God to create an immediacy of religious experience. Marsh's diary provides evidence of this in its documentation of the roller-coaster relationship between Marsh and his God. At some points Marsh came close to despair, noting 'O Lord how vain is my Life that in many days I can discern nothing remarkable in it my good Days are soon numbered', or asking 'have there been no remarkable occurrences between my God & me all this while?' At other points he exults in 'holy raptures & divine communions'.[23] While Marsh makes few references to what sustained this spiritual life, it seems from one comment in May 1692 that the sacrament of Holy Communion was 'to the great comfort of mine own soul' and constituted renewal of his personal covenant with God.[24]

The outworking of this powerful spirituality can be seen in Marsh's involvement with the campaign for moral reform and religious renewal spearheaded by the Societies for the Reformation of Manners in Dublin during the 1690s.[25] In 1695, the year after his appointment to the see of Dublin, Marsh wrote to his episcopal friend William Lloyd outlining the spiritual progress made since he came to the diocese. In the rural parts of the diocese the Eucharist was celebrated five or six times a year, as opposed to the canonically required thrice, although Marsh wanted to increase the frequency to a monthly celebration. In Dublin city the monthly communion had become a weekly one in the most populous parishes and fortnightly in the remainder. He also wished that some city churches would institute daily prayers, hoping that this would spread to the surrounding countryside, but he expected rural parishes at least to institute prayers on Wednesdays and Fridays. Similar reforms were instituted in the diocese of Armagh when he moved there.[26] He encouraged the Societies for the Reformation of Manners and provided £40 for the establishment of a weekly lecture in the city to improve moral standards.[27] He harnessed the expanding world of print in Dublin to convey his message of moral and religious reformation. He had 2,500 copies of one of Archbishop Tillotson's sermons printed to be distributed free to householders within the diocese through the parish clergy. He also distributed 'several thousand' small books of devotions to encourage family and personal prayer and funded the publication of a sermon by Thomas Pollard, Rector of St Peter's in Dublin, on the subject of family prayer. In addition he composed a new catechism for the use of the diocese which was printed in 1699.[28] While the pious Accomptant General, James Bonnell, had reservations about the low-key way in which all this was done he could not complain about the result, observing in 1696 that Marsh 'sets heartily to promote religion and piety and calls upon his friends to give him what helps they can towards it which though he be no active man yet will have some good.'[29] All this testifies to what Marsh's narrative also proclaims: the reality of religion as a powerful set of beliefs which shaped the life of Narcissus Marsh.

While the original narrative compiled by Marsh in December 1690 is highly revealing about the mental world of Narcissus Marsh, the entries he added to it over the next six years are much less about spiritual health and motivations and more about the public face of a senior churchman. They contain his account of the minutiae of the stormy parliament of 1692, especially as it affected the church, and that of 1695–97. Although Marsh had been a bishop since 1682, these were his first experiences of attending parliament in the House of Lords, because parliament had not met since 1666 apart from the Jacobite parliament of 1689, which Marsh did not attend. For Marsh this was a sharp learning curve. Since Primate Boyle was too incapacitated to give any leadership in the church, much of the work fell to Marsh and Vesey as the two archbishops present. This was not a world that Marsh much liked. He declared in 1700 that 'worldly business is that which above all things I do hate'.[30] As someone who was primarily a scholar, and a scholar motivated by a deep sense of religious piety, he wished to be left to the world of books. When business overwhelmed him after being appointed a Lord Justice in 1699 he proclaimed defiantly that 'I am resolv'd to have something to do with books still as long as I live.'[31] Marsh was not an adept administrator which may go some way to explaining his dislike of business. He was certainly conscious of his limitations, as he wrote after one of his first periods as Lord Justice: 'I have found by experience how ill qualified I am for the well discharging of so great a trust as that of having a share in the government of this kingdom.'[32] While Swift's description of Marsh, printed as Appendix 4 below, may have much of the caricature about it, it does contain an important insight, that Marsh was ill at ease in the world when manipulating patronage and striking political deals. The pious James Bonnell agreed, declaring in 1695 that 'The present Archbishop of Dublin, Dr Marsh, formerly provost of ye College, is certainly a very pious good man and a scholar but weak and bookish and guided by others.'[33] Bonnell's friend William King, then Bishop of Derry, expressed similar sentiments in 1697, noting that 'The archbishop of Dublin (though an excellent scholar) yet is too modest and unacquainted with the world to make a great bustle without which I am informed little is done there.'[34]

Despite being temperamentally unsuited to the world of parliament or administration, Marsh found administrative duties thrust upon him, especially after his appointment as Archbishop of Dublin in 1694. Archbishop Boyle's senility and near-blindness meant that Marsh did a great deal of the preparatory work for the parliament, and the problems he encountered were noted his diary. Despite his obvious dislike of the task, Marsh shouldered much of this burden in an attempt to introduce much-needed reform into the Irish church for, as he put it, 'ye better establishment of this poor distressed church'.[35] As with the more congenial world of scholarship, what motivated Marsh to undertake these uncongenial tasks was a sense of religious duty. He noted in 1701 that such tasks came because God's 'providence hath ordered them to be' and God would 'by his almighty power enable me to act so as may make most for His glory and his majesty's real service'.[36] As he wrote of parliamentary committees in his diary for 10 October 1692, 'The Lord enable me to discharge my duty therein to his honour & Glory.'[37] He repeatedly asked for God's protection as crises loomed in parliament. This religious dimension of duty helps to explain why he took his administrative duties seriously. He was actively concerned about the quality of the bishops appointed to the church. He rejoiced when a godly reformer such as Nathaniel Foy became a bishop, but recorded his sense of relief that he was not a party to the consecration of William Fitzgerald, a nephew of Archbishop Boyle, and tried to block the appointment of Edward Walkington as Bishop of Down and Connor in 1695 on the grounds that he was lazy, he kept company with low people such as soldiers, and frequented coffee-houses.[38] Not only was Marsh aware of his duties and impelled by the religious impulse to fulfil them, however unsuccessfully, he also reminded others of their duty which he considered they had an obligation to carry out. He harried some of the Lord Justices into a more public manifestation of their religious practice so that they would provide an example to the lower social orders.[39] Marsh's concern with his administrative duties, like his promotion of moral reformation or the pursuit of scholarship, sprang from his intense spirituality, dramatically revealed in this diary.

Narcissus Marsh was in many ways an unusual, indeed peculiar, figure. If Jonathan Swift's description of him reproduced in Appendix 4 is even partially true, it suggests a man characterised by eccentricity rather than wit or ability in the world of affairs. His standing is not improved by comparisons with a younger generation of ecclesiastical high-flying reformers with whom he overlapped, most importantly Archbishop William King and Bishop Nathaniel Foy of Waterford. Marsh lacked their political acumen and administrative ability in the service of the church, preferring instead the more restrained world of scholarship as a way of glorifying God. His political shortcomings should not cast doubts on the sincerity of his religious convictions or the influence of his spiritual experiences as a driving force in his life. The spiritual lives of most of those who lived in seventeenth-century Ireland are virtually a closed book to us today. In the case of a select few we can catch a glimpse of the reality of religion in that world. The diary of Narcissus Marsh offers, if not a spotlight, at least a candle to illuminate the soul of a scholar bishop.

Editorial Note

The autograph manuscript of Narcissus Marsh's diary has not survived. The text as printed here is taken from a mid-eighteenth-century transcript of the document which is now in Marsh's Library, Dublin, MS Z2. 2. 3. How accurate that transcript is it is impossible to say. It does seem clear that the transcriber modernised the text to a limited extent. In letters of the 1690s Marsh invariably uses 'ym' for 'them', but in the surviving text this has been modernised. On the other hand, many of the features of Marsh's orthography, such as '&' for 'and', have been preserved, which does suggest a careful transcriber. The hand of the copyist has not been firmly identified, but it shows strong similarities with that of William Fletcher, who was prebendary of St Michael's in Christ Church, 1747–49, prebendary of Tymothan in St Patrick's, 1750–73, and successively Treasurer, Precentor and Dean of Kildare. If he was the transcriber, then a good deal of trust may be placed in the copy, since he was also involved in the transcription of the medieval deeds of Christ Church in the 1740s known as the *Registrum Novum*, which attains a very high standard of accuracy indeed.

The texts printed in the narrative and the appendices have not been modernised. In cases where words are missing or where expansion of contractions has seemed necessary this has been done within square brackets. A few sentences occasionally appear in the margin of the narrative and these have been placed in the main text, where they seem to belong, within angle brackets. Passages underlined in the text have been given italics in this edition. Dates in the text have not been modernised, though in a few instances year dates have been identified in square brackets as old style [o.s.] or new style [n.s.] for the sake of clarity, and in the introduction the year has been taken as beginning on 1 January rather than 25 March as in Marsh's diary.

The Recollections and Diary of Narcissus Marsh 1638–1696

[Marsh's Library, Dublin, MS Z2. 2. 3]

Narcissus Marsh Borne Dec[r] 20th	1638
Entered Commoner in Magdalen Hall Oxford	1654
Comenced Batchelor lent 1658 & June 29 made fellow of E[xeter] C[ollege]	
Comenced Master of Arts; at the act	1660
Consecrated Deacon & Priest March	1662
Comenced Batchelor of Divinity Mich[aelmas]	1667
Doctor	1671
Principal of S[t] Albans Hall, Ma[rch] 12	1673
Provost of Trinity Colledge Dublin Jan[uary] 24	1678
Bishop of Leighlin & Fernes Consecrated May 6	1683
Arch Bishop of Cashell Dec[r] 25	1691
Arch Bishop of Dublin May 24	1694
A.B: of Armagh, L[ord] P[rimate] of all I[reland]: Feb[y] 18	1702
Died Nov[r] 2[d] 1713 Buried in St Patricks Dublin	
Lord Justice of Ireland	1699 1701 1702 1706 1707 1711

A DIARY DECEMR 20, 1690

In the name of God The Father, Son & Holy Ghost, Amen being this Evening at six of the Clock newly entered upon the 52d year of my Age, of which time (tho' I have used my Utmost endeavours to improve it to the best advantage of my studies which I always minded without any regard had to ye world, or the things thereof) being conscious to myself that much hath been spent in vanity, I think it behoves me now *to begin to number my days that I may apply my heart unto wisdom*,[1] & in order to it, I shall take a brief prospect of my former Life.

I was born on St Thomas's Eve, Decr 20, 1638, in a village called Hanington, near Highworth, in the north part of Wiltshire, of honest parents, my father's name Wm Marsh, my Mother's Grace Colburn, of an honest family of that name in Dorsetshire. My father lived upon his own Estate worth upward of £60 per annum & designing to breed me up to learning (though I was the Youngest of five Children Vizt two Daughters and three Sons, to all which especially the Sons he gave good Education) he first put me to one Mr Lamb who taught a small school in the same parish; then to Mr Virgil Pleydall at Lyshill near adjoining, next to Mr Dudley a Minister at Highworth, where I began to learn Latin. Afterwards to Mr Crouch Minister of Hanington & lastly about the year 1652 unto Mr Thos Hedges Minister of Rodburne in Wiltshire, in all which schools I never was so much as once whipt or beaten. <In this time I narrowly escaped drowning. God make me for ever thankfull for that great mercy, & O Lord reward him that saved my Life.>

I was Entered Commoner in Magdalen Hall in Oxford at the act in 1654, being 15 Years old & an half and having been hurt by the bite of a dog I came not to reside there untill May ye 10 following 1655. <When undergraduate I had a dangerous fall from a horse at Rodburn. Lord make me thankfull for ye deliverance.> I betook myself seriously to the study of old Philosophy, Mathematicks and oriental languages, and before Lent 1658 (when I took my degree of Batchelor of arts) I had made a good progress in them all. I was then 19 Year's old & about a quarter. All this while I constantly kept an entire fast every week, from Thursday six a Clock at night untill Saturday eleven at Noon. For wch God's name be praised. It happened that the same Lent I performed my exercise of answering with one Mr John Jenner of Wildhill in Wiltshire under The moderation of Mr Fido Chaplain Fellow of Exeter College then Ma[ster] of the Schools, my performance pleased Mr Fido so well that a Wiltshire fellowship in Exeter College (whereof there are two) being then void, & by a fortunate concurrence of causes I being occasionally named & recommended as a person fit for that fellowship by my friend Mr John Jenner unto one Mr Hitchcock then fellow of Lincoln College (who at ye request of the fellows of Exeter College, made enquiry abroad for a fit person for that fellowship, they then having no one, either of that or of any other college, in their Eye, that they liked) as soon as Mr Fido understood this he appeared so much my friend & recomended me so heartily to the Revd Dr John Conant[2] then Rector & to the rest of the fellows, that after a diligent & frequent examination I was thereupon chosen fellow of ye sd College, on St Peter's Day, June ye 29th or the morrow June the 30: 1658 & this laid the foundation of what I now am. The Lord reward Mr Fido (if yet alive) & his posterity & friends for his great kindness to me.

As for my friend Mr J: Jenner being fallen into poverty, I have already paid above £2000 Debts for him: & if God shall enable me will do more for him yet & Not think I can do enough for him, that hath been so kind to me. The Lord give him a Heart to make good use of it. To his kindness, together with thy mercy & goodness, O Lord, do I owe what I am; Enable me therefore O God to return his kindness back again upon him, I beseech Thee, and remember me for Good, my Lord & my God.[3]

I was still sedulous in my study, being more desirous to know truth, than to engage in worldly business, & especially in the vanity of conversation. At the act 1660 (being 21 years old & a half) I proceeded Master of arts (having term given me; as I had likewise in the degree of

Batchelor of arts, which then was usual, but never practised since). Henceforward I remitted nothing of my studies as far as I could for attending offices in the College & Pupills (of whom I had many & I thank my God, that my conscience doth not reproach me for any negligence either in my study or calling, but I do find a great deal of comfort in what I have done.[)]

In March 1662 (being then a little past 23 years of Age) I was Invited up to London to take the living of Swindon in Wiltshire, that was then void & in the King's Gift. In order whereunto I was put into full orders at one & the same time by Dr Skinner Bp of Oxford, in K. Henry ye 7th Chappel Westminster, though then under age for Priesthood. The Lord forgive us both, but then I knew no better but that it might Legally be done.

I took the living (procured for me by Mr Math Wren[4] Eldest Son to Bp Wren, Secretary to My Lord Chancellor Hyde) & presently after Dr Seth Ward[5] being made Bp of Exeter, he chose me to be his Chaplain. But preferring my study to all worldly advantages, I still stuck close to the university.

Being hindered in getting into possession of the living of Swindon (Mr Violet a Gentleman of ye parish laying claim to ye right of presenting)[6] after I had peaceable possesion, finding that the Marrying a Gentlewoman would be expected from me by those, on whose favour I had already & must much depend & being averse to ye Entangling myself in the cares of the world (but indeed & chiefly my father being averse to it, without wch I had done it but without him I would do nothing) I at once resolutely broke the chains & quitted the living, after I had peaceably Enjoyed it a year & adhered to my fellowship, keeping in the College all along.

I had suffered some threats before from F.B. about the Woman and the B[ishop] of E[xeter] had laboured to bring about his & her design; but when they saw 'twould not do, & that I had quitted the living & broken all their measures, the first threatned High & the B[ishop] of E[xeter] remanded his Instrumt for Chaplainship, which I very willingly sent him.

O my God, I bless thy holy Name for delivering me out of the snare that they had laid for me;[7] & if I have done amiss in that affair, I beg thy pardon, I beg their pardon, & am ready to make my satisfaction. & O Lord pardon them I beseech Thee for what they designed & what they acted (not agst me I do think but) agst the intent & purpose of my heart to render Thee & thy holy Church such service as in a marry'd state I could not be able to do, wch is ye only reason why I have hitherto kept myself a single man: tho God in his providence has so ordered affairs, by reason of Engagem^{ts} I have lain under, that I could not be so serviceable in my station as I proposed to myself & designed to be. The Lord my God enable me henceforth to be so that I may in this respect also redeem my time.

Before this in the year 1664 I preached my first Sermon at St Mary's in Oxford before the University, & the 5th of Novr next ye Anniversary Thanksgiving sermon for that great deliverance & the next Lent after (being that year Proproctor of the University) I preacht a Lent sermon at St Peters in ye East, in Oxford.

I had also before this betaken myself to the practice of musick, especially of the Bass Viol, & after the fire of London, I constantly kept a weekly consort (of Instrumental musick & sometimes vocal) in my Chamber on Wednesday in the afternoon, & then on Thursday, as long as I lived in Oxford.

This I did as an exercise, using no other, but labouring harder at my study all the rest of the week.

Yet O Lord I beseech thee to forgive me this loss of time and vain Conversation.

In the year 1665 when King Charles was in Oxford, at the request of my worthy friend Sr John Ernle (of Berrytown in Wiltshire; since one of the Commissioners of the King's Customs, then Chancellor of the Exchequer & Commissioner of the Treasurey, but now turned out of all by King William) I was made Chaplain to my Lord Chancellor Hyde,[8] before whom I preached in Worcester house the May following; & in Berkshire house the February after that. He advised me to continue in Oxford & follow my study & he would provide for me being his Countryman, but he did not continue in England long enough to do it after that.

And so I was again brought to depend upon my fellowship & industry, from that & my Pupils picking up a good maintenance & indeed hitherto I had never gotten anything any other way, because I could never think of leaving the University untill I should have finished my course of studies and was become Dr in Divinity, And therefore I never sought for any preferment, nor would I accept of any either out of the University or in it, that would have taken me off from my Studies.

In 1667 Mich[aelma]s Term I took my degree of Batchelor in Divinity being then about 29 Years old. so about this time & after I had many advantageous offers for marriage. One <Mr P's daughter> who had £800 to her portion, another <Mr N's daughter> £1500, another £2400, and another <E: Cin Oxford's lovely daughter who died soon after> of meaner fortune than either, but all very desirable (I might rather have said beautiful, lovely persons), yet I waved all these considerations & all thoughts of marriage for the reasons above mentioned.

The Lord remember me for Good.

About this time Mrs Pleydall of Ammy offered to bring me in to be domestick Chaplain to Sr Orlando Bridgman,[9] then Lord Keeper, to whom her sister was married, his then Chaplain Dr Frampton being to be made Dean of Gloucester (who is now Bp of ye same) but I refused it, resolving not to live Chaplain in any mans house, lest it might rob me of too much time from my dear studies which I would not part with for any preferment & therefore I desired & cared for none.

Remember me O my God.

About this time also I became acquainted with that excellent man & good patron Dr John Fell,[10] then Dean of Christ Church & afterwards Bp of Oxford, whose memory is pretious.

O Lord think upon his good Works & Labour of Love.

In the year 1671 at Act I commenced Dr of Divnity being aged 32 years & an half, but my Lectures for my degree were not read untill Mich[aelma]s term after when I read 6 solemn lectures on this subject *De Legibus Divinis* [Concerning the Laws of God] the reason of the delay was, that being by Dr Fell engaged to correct ye translations of Basamon and Zonaras's Comments on the Canons of the Greek Councils wch Mr Beveridge was Then printing at the Theater in Oxford,[11] & to revise his notes &c, & to supervise the whole work, I could not possibly get time to compose my Lectures untill that work was finished or very nigh done, it having taken up my whole time for above a year before, in wch I had nothing but the honour & satisfaction of serving the publick. Lord remember me for this.

I still continued a Tutor in Exeter College in wch Imploymt I found delight & much advantage as to my studies.

Some Years before this I began at Leisure hours to revise, alter & adjust Du Trien's Logick, & make it fitter for use. I printed that Logick with additions some years after at Oxford, & then having pared off what I thought superfluous in the first book I altered & changed & added very much to it but so as to bring it into a lesser Volume and make it quite a new book: I printed it here in Dublin for the use of Trinity College.[12]

In 1673 May 12 being then past 34 years old I was made principal of Alban Hall in Oxford by the Duke of Ormond then Chancellor of the University at the Intercession of Dr Blandford Bp of Worcester and Dr Fell Dean of Christ Church in Oxford, Dr Lamplugh the then Principal (now ABp of York) resigning it up to me, where I lived 5 years & 8 Months and continued a Tutor all ye time & moderated disputations in the Hall myself, by wch means I acquired a greater number of Scholars than could be lodged in the hall, having always above 60 in Commons.

In that Interval I printed du Triens Logick before mentioned, & in three weeks time & consideration composed a little Tract concerning ye *Sympathy of Viol or Lute Strings*, at Dr Plots request, who hath printed the same in his natural history of Oxfordshire.[13]

I also calculated the Lines of the planetary motions, & that described by the nail in a cart wheel, & got them Engraven but have not yet printed them.

In the beginning of March 1677 Dr Fell Bp of Oxford made me the offer of the Provostship of Trinity College near Dublin in Ireland when it should be void. & this offer he made me from the Duke of Ormond, then Lord Lieutenant of that Kingdom. I embraced the offer & the place becoming void in Decem^{r} next by the promotion of Dr Ward the then Provost to the Bpk of Ossory;[14] I left Oxford Decr 23: 1678 being then 40 Years old and two days & arrived at Dublin January the 19th after, & was sworn & invested Provost Jany 24: 1678.

But finding this place very troublesome partly by reason of ye multitude of business & impertinent[15] Visits the Provost is oblidged to, & partly by reason of the ill Education that the young Scholars have before they come to the College, whereby they are both rude & ignorant; I was Quickly weary of 340 Youngmen & boys in this lewd debauch'd town; & the more so because I had no time to follow my allways dearly beloved studies.[16] This I represented to My Lord Arran, then Lord Deputy of Ireland, in the absence of his Father the Duke of Ormond, then in England. He immediately wrote to the Duke concerning me, who returned a gracious answer, as he afterwards told me.

In this time I printed the forementioned Logick as I had digested it from Du Trien & others & published it in Dublin for the use of Trinity College.

About Christmas 1682 the Bprick of Leighlin & ffernes, becoming void by the Death of Bp Boyle, My Lord Arran recommended me for it without my knowledge, & in February following his Majestys letter came for it & I took out my Patent being 44 Years old & about two Months; but I was not consecrated untill the 6th of May following, because being required to continue the Governm^{t} of the College untill Dr Huntington[17] should come over to assume it, wch I could not well do without his Majesty's dispensation, that was thought most proper to be before my consecration, I deferred untill my dispensation came.

In the following Winter 1683, was set up the Philosophical meeting in Dublin that met & formed itself into a society in the Provost's Lodgings.[18] There at the first opening of it, as a Prelude to what we were to do, I in 3 or 4 Days time composed an *Introductory discourse to the Doctrine of Sands* [*sic*], which was sent to the Society in Oxford & then printed in the *Philosophical Transactions*.[19]

I continued quiet in my Bprick untill K: James came to the Crown, repairing Churches, planting Curates where wanting & doing what good I could; but in a little time the Irish Papists grew headstrong and began to be very uneasy to us.

When they had taken out new Charters, threatening to throw down a[ll] the inclosures of old Leighlin I opposed them; for which I was summoned before the Council-board, but came off well. A narrative whereof I have amongst my papers.[20] This was in Mich[aelma]s term 1688. For this the Irish thereabout bare me a Grudge.

About the 10th or 12th day of Jany following a troop of horse & two Companies of foot beset my house at midnight, pretending to search for arms & for my Lord Coloony; but in truth t'was for me, who was gone to Dublin two days before. Thy Name be praised O Lord, for this preservation.

Upon complaint to my Lord Tyrconnell, then Lord Deputy, ye Captn is Cashiered, hereupon the Irish threaten me more severely & openly. I dare not return to my house in the Country, but stay in the Provosts Lodgings in the College.

1688 in the latter end of February or beginning of March the Protestants are disarmed, & 2 Companies of foot keep guard in the College for 2 Days. Now all things being in a desperate condition, & I not daring to go home & not being able to continue in the Provost's Lodgings, wch his Kinswoman Mrs Denys had quitted & disposed of his goods, nor having money to maintain myself in the City; having obtained my Lord Tyrconnell's leave, I went for England that March & strait for London, where I was kindly rec^{d} by the Abp of Canterbury, the Abp of York, the Bp of London &c: but especially by the Bp of St Asaph,[21] who bestowed upon me the parish of Gresford for my support under that Calamity, which I do yet enjoy; & by the Bp of Salisbury Dr Burnet,[22] who earnestly invited me several times to be at his house untill I might return for Ireland. The Bp of Lincoln[23] also presented me with 5 Guineas the Lord reward them all for their kindness to the distressed.

After 4 Months stay in London having in the meantime made provision for as many poor Clergymen of Ireland that were forced out thence as I could I went to Oxford, being invited thither by Dr Bury Rector of Exeter College, where I was kindly entertained for 9 Months & furnished with all necessaries both by the Dr & his wife & by Mrs Guise her Daughter. The Lord reward them for it.

The Bp of London sent me 20 Gues, Mr Rowney sent me 5 Guineas Mrs Bury offered 20 Gus at my departure, but I refused them, as having no present occasion.

1689.

The first Sunday in Mich[aelm]ass Term I preached before the University in St Mary's Church, on 1 Cor 1.20. *Where is the wise &c.*

1690.

April I return'd to London. The 3d Wednesday in June I preached before the Queen at Whitehall, the King being gone to Ireland. The 3d Wednesday in July I came for Ireland, & arrived at Dublin August ye 3d, with some danger and Difficulty; as I also had in going for England being like to be cast away by the Vessel's striking on the Sand. God's Holy Name be forever praised for these & all his mercys; for his preserving me for Good Peoples support.

Especially for the kindness shew'd me by the Bps of London, Lincoln, St Asaph, Salisbury; by Mr Rowney, Dr Bury & his wife, who have been wondrously bountifull to me, but above all Mrs Guise whose unspeakable kindness & bounty to me must never be forgotten.

Lord remember them all for good & shower down thy blessings both Temporal and Spiritual upon them. Deliver Dr B[ury] out of all his troubles and comfort Mrs B[ury] & G[uise] with the Comforts of thy right & of thy left hand; O Lord bring them safe to thine Eternal Kingdom.

Since my last coming to Ireland I have done but little besides bewailing the miseries of this poor Country. *O that my head were water & my eyes a fountain of Tears.*[24]

And being now come to the place & time where I began I proceed.

1690.

Decr 20. Yesterday the certain news of his Majesty's design of Translating me to the Abprick of Cashell being arrived, wch was this day confirmed. The first act I did was a Deed of Charity, in remitting near £30 to a poor Widow in a Fine, God be thanked for inclining my heart thereto.[25]

Decr 21 was spent in Devotion to the comfort of my Soul God grant I may enjoy many such Days.

Decr 22. I promoted Mr Andrew Nesbit to the parishes of Bally Adam & Fontstown in the Queen's County upon Thos Fitzgeralds quitting them and turning Papist. I pray God make him serviceable in that place & Instrumental to the saving many Souls.

23^{d}

Was spent in writing to the Bps of London, St Asaph, Salisbury, Abp of Tuam, Dr Tilllotson dean of St Pauls, Sr St John Broderick, Mr Minshull Jeweller, my brother, M^{r} Fr: Evans Secretary to ye Bp of St Asaph. This Evening I found out a solution of a third of the 5 difficult Cases, wherein *one side with the sum of the other two & one angle being given in A Triangle, the rest are required*; as 5 Days before I had found out another, & this time twelve months in Oxford I had found out another. The Lord be praised for thus inlightning my understanding & be pleased to continue to do so daily.

24.

I rec^{d} money unexpectedly, God be thanked. had an untoward dream. Lord preserve me from such & grant me more such that tend to piety & thy fear, as I have often had, one especially concerning the day of Judgment I must here write down for my memory's sake, tho after above 20 years 'tis now as fresh in my mind as ever. I dreamed that I saw my Saviour Sitting on his Throne & several brought to Judgment, before him, among others a maid condemned for making measure of Ale in her Quart pots; at Lenth a notorious bloody Villain, a thief & a robber, at whose appearance the Devils (who peeped in from below thro a little door like the hazard in a Tennis Court) roared & seemed to strive amongst themselves who should enter first through that door into the place of Judgm[t] to seize on him[,] whom being condemned one of them presently Reaching in caught him by the wastband of his breeches behind pluckd him into them & gave him a whirle down into hell, at this whole action of the Devils & their bolting in to lay hold on the Malefactor (of whose terror I have so fresh an Idea at this time that I tremble to think of it) behind affrighted I ran behind our Saviour's Chair, who rose up from his Seat, turned about, took me, & embraced me kindly, & pressing me hard between his Arms against his breast said *now thou shalt see how dear my Love is to thee*, and presently after that I awoke in the most heavenly rapture of Love to my Saviour, that ever I was in, in my life. O Blessed Jesus, continue this thy Love to me, increase my Love to thee & let me both sleeping & waking enjoy many & many of those holy raptures & divine communions with thee my Saviour & redeemer.

About the same time or not many years distant from it I had another pretty strange dream (I think it was about 23 Years ago) Viz[t] that riding through London Street after my good friend S[r] John Ernle, I met a man in black of a lively brisk aspect (whose Idea I have now perfect in my mind. I never yet saw any man quite like him but my Lord Brounker was the nearest like of any one) he walking very fast with his hat cock'd, made a sudden stop when he came just up to me, look'd me steadfastly in the face & said *Salve Episcope Granatensis* [Greetings, O Bishop of Granada]. I demanded Quisnam Ego [Who, pray? I?] He reply'd Imo tu [Yes, indeed you], & went on, as before. I also rode on musing how this should be true, what (said I to myself) shall I turn Papist, or shall the King of England conquer Spain & with this finding I had lost S[r] John Ernle I was at a stand when out of a house came 3 or 4 friars in their habits saluted me after the same manner, earnestly invited me in which I accepted of, found a large table well furnisht, said Grace at their importunity, both before & after meat, but cautiously, took leave of them & waked. I then little thought (tho I dreamed[)] of being ABp.

Another Dream I had about the same time, that I was in Rome, saw the Pope carried into S[t] Peter's Church on men's shoulders before whom all fell on their knees as he past by; but I shifted from place to place in the Church to avoid it & being taken notice of; but at last seeing I was observed & eyed by some that watched me, I privately got out of the Church, & entering a house fell into the Company of learned men; who raising a discourse concerning religion, to ensnare or detect me, as I apprehended, I replied thereto with so much subtilty & maintained the dispute with so much dexterity (defending truth & yet giving them no advantage against me) that when I awaked I did much admire myself for the subtileness & acuteness of my Answers which I did then remember perfectly well, being able to do nothing like it when I was Waking, And indeed tis wonderfull that a man's reason should act so strongly when he is sleeping; unless we look upon such dreams to come from God as many of them do.

Lord guide me sleeping as well as waking that my night dreams as well as my Day thoughts may be thine, both from thee & to thee.

25.

I rec^d the Holy Comunion in the Coll. Chappel, where Dr Huntingdon the Provost preached. the Lord make it comfortable to my Soul & enable me to perform my vows that I have now renewed.

26.

This day I found out the solution of the two other Cases of the Triangle before mentioned. O Lord thy holy name be for ever praised for thus enlightening my understanding & discovering to me hidden Truths, thine be the Glory & continue thou more & more to enlighten my mind & let me in the way of truth, especially unto true saving knowledge Amen, Amen. This night I had a dream that much troubled me. Lord ever more keep me that no such thing really happen me, *For thine is the power.*[26]

27.

This day was all spent in reflecting on my former life, & drawing the foregoing account of it. Lord make me often & seriously to reflect on what is past & prepare me for what is to come.

28. 29. 30.

I served God & followed my Study; but did no good deed. God be thanked for the 2 first & pardon the last.

29.

I attended the Provost & fellows to the Lord Justice Porters[27] at Clancartys house, where Mr Reader (one of the senior fellows) made a Latin Speech to congratulate his arrival here & association into the Governm^t^, the other two Justices being my Lord Sidney and Mr Coningsby.[28]

31.

Wrote to the Bp of St Asaph, sent a Copy of ye King's letter for ye Abprick of Cashell.

January 1: 1690 [1691 n.s.].

I wrote to the Bps of London, St Asaph, Salisbury, & to Dr Tillotson Dean of St Paul's.

2.

Rec^d^ a letter from the Bp of Salisbury, dated Decr 20, giving an acc^t^ of a discourse in England of letters to be sent to the King of France from the discontented party in England to invite him to send 30000 men next Spring when a considerable number in England would join. Nae hominum insania servitutis, imo Tyrannidis imo papismi poene, aboreo hic revocandi amantissimorum, cupidissimorum. Faxit Deus ut tandem Sapiamus & libertatorem vere, unanimitus & serie agnoscamus. Hoc Deus, Hoc patria & parentes hoc religio vere christiana, hoc proximi & confaederati, hoc Coelum Terraque, quin & conscientia clamant expectantque, Det Deus ut fiat.[29] [I truly abjure those men's madness who are so eager and desirous of reinstating here what is slavery, or rather tyranny, namely the dreadful outworkings of Popery. God ordains it that, in the end, we all know and acknowledge Him together as the true liberator. This is what God, this is what our country and our forefathers, this is what the truly Christian religion, this is what our neighbours and allies, this is what heaven and earth, to say nothing of conscience, all cry out for and await. May God grant that it be so.]

I had a dream that afflicted me much. God preserve me.

3.

This Day a Corporal of the Militia of Dublin was secured for having taken 5 Guineas of a fellow to let him into town the night before when he was upon the Guard the Lord preserve us.

News came also that we had taken the Bridge of Lanesborough that the Irish rapparees had ravaged about Kilcullen Bridge & plundered my Lord Primates house at Blessinton. God be merciful to us & preserve Dublin now that they dare come within eleven miles of it.

I had another bad dream Lord have mercy upon me.

6.

God blessed me with the invention of a way to find out (& express) any number of middle proportionals betwixt any two numbers, as betwixt 1 & 2 thus —

7.

After great Study I had a good invention in Conical Sections, for which Gods holy name be praised.

11.

Wee had news of a discovery made In England of practices wth France wherein my Lord Preston was concerned & being taken in a Ship ready to set sail thither, was committed to the Tower at London for high Treason. my Lord Clarendon was also committed.[30]

16.

God forgive me that I have done or thought nothing memorable for some days past. The King went towards Holland the 6th Ins^t^, my Lords Clarendon & Preston clapt up in the Tower for high Treason & Ashton & Elliot into Newgate for the same reason because they sent to invite the King of France to send 20000 foot into Scotland wth Arms & many from England would join them. A fish bone sticking in my throat this night at supper, I had a great deliverance by speedily bringing it up again; for which God's holy name be praised.

20.

I wrote to the Bps of Worcester & Oxford.

22.

I united [*sic*] a difficult knott in Algebra; for wch I praise the Allmighty — Sic Spiritu suo quotidie illuminet mentem meam. Sed Gratiae & scientiae Authorem illum semper confiteat ego et agnoscam [May He so enlighten my mind every day by His Spirit. But may I for my part always recognise and acknowledge that He is the source of grace and understanding].

The night before I had a grateful dream Viz^t^. that I was walking up a pleasant ascent (being a green lane with a considerable rising at the upper End more than all the way) at the top whereof was paradise or the seat of the Blessed (having my Sister with me) but was furiously assaulted by Cerberus (whom I forced into the river that ran on the right side of that lane & made him pass to the other side) & threaten'd by the Fiends all along but went on couragiously without any fear of them, untill at length I unfortunately awaked before I got to the top of the lane or hill at the upper End of it. Lord enable me at length to arrive at the Top of the mount of God that place of rest & bliss, that was shewed me in this vision (wch I desire always to remember) but is not to be found in this Vale here below, how pleasant soever it may seem.

24.

I wrote to the Bps of London and St Asaph & to M^r^ Fr: Evans &c. Trouble & anguish have taken hold upon me, thou art my Saviour & redeemer make no long Tarrying O my God.

25.

O Lord how vain is my Life, that in many days I can discern nothing remarkable in it my good Days are soon numbered.

This day Dr King,[31] Dean of St Patrick's, Bp elect of Derry was consecrated at Christchurch in Dublin; oh do thou enable him to promote thy Glory in the salvation of Souls.

30.

His Majesty's warrant for my Translation to Cashell dated Decr 25 came hither a former Warrant having been granted Decr 11 but was laid by because imperfect. O Lord make me always to bear in mind the mightiness of thy Charge that I have undertaken.

Two Ships from England were this night cast away in ye mouth of ye harbour at Dublin or very near it & several persons drowned. Lord make us ever thankful who are hitherto preserved alive.

31.

I wrote to the Bp of St Asaph & Dr Tillotson[32] in behalf of Dr Huntington P[rovost of] T[rinity] C[ollege] to be the next Bp here in Ireland.

Feby 17.

Many Days have I been sleeping rather than waking, rather dead than alive, so insignificant hath my life been. Lord pardon & praised be thy name that when I was in a streight for money to pass my patent for the ABprick of Cashell, thou didst raise up a friend for me in England, who sent me money hither without any seeking, yea unknown to me, as she had furnished me with considerable sums before of her own free bounty. Reward her O Lord for her bounty, Charity, & labour of Love & may her Soul live for ever.

March 5.

I have gone on hitherto in the same condition. Lord have mercy upon me. I wrote to Sr Jeffery Shakery of Gwenfyl & Mr Jasper Peck of Trevallyne both in the parish of Gresford concerning the tythes thereof & the paym^{t} of the Curates Mr Atkinson & Mr Floyd's sallary, I having quitted that parish Jan: 18 before my patent for Cashell sealed.

6.

My heart is fixed O Lord, my heart is fixed, even on thee my God,[33] Oh grant that it may continue so as long as I live.

8. This day was Bartholomew Vigors L.L.D. consecrated Bp of Leighlin & Fernes, upon the taking out my Patent for the ABprick of

Cashell which was done on thursday March 5, In w[ch] there was this unhappy circumstance, that S[r] Charles Porter one of the Lords Justices & Lord Chancellor of Ireland, having of his own head raised the fees for passing the broad seal (in those miserable times) from three Cobs for the recepi (which were formerly paid) for a Bp to 5 Guineas & for an ABp to 10 Guineas & to his purse bearer Eight pounds, w[ch] sums being resolved never to pay but rather to Petition the King thereupon, & for that purpose had ordered my Patent to be stopt, nevertheless Richard Jones of Bridestreet went fraudulently & laid down the fees & took out my Patent by which means there being a Precedent set, those unjust & exacting fees will for ever be kept up to the great prejudice of all Patentees of Ireland & the Eternal reproach of S[r] Charles Porter the first setter up of them w[ch], I call God to witness I opposed as much as I could, & would have been content to have lost my Bprick & my Life too, rather than have submitted thereto (had I not been knavishly circumvented by the means before mentioned) & this purely for the sake of all those that shall come after me. Oh Lord be Thou my Strenth & my support.[34] Enable me always successfully to oppose all manner of vice & especially Usurpations and Oppressions & oh Lord bring all the practicers of them to a true sense of their Error & amendment of life & give us all patience to bear these amongst other Calamities that thou hast laid upon us of this poor distressed Kingdom thy will be done.[35]

9.

Make me O Lord, to continue still in the same mind, to pray for mine oppressors & for whose by those means we all suffer, that God will turn their hearts to himself from evil doing Lord look down in compassion upon this distressed Kingdom.

14.

I wrote to M[r] Verman, M[rs] B[ury] & G[uise] at Exeter College.
I am thine O Lord, save me for thy mercy's Sake!

16.

My God, My God look upon me with pity & compassion, forgive y[e]

Sins of this & all the days past of my Life. Oh thou Holy one of Israel[36] I am thine, O Save me for thy Mercy's sake.

21.

I wrote to Mr Dalton of Waterford, to Mr Leake of Cashell[37] & to the Bp of Leighlin.

22.

I preached before the Lords Justices at Christchurch in Dublin, on Rom: 8:13. Lord I beseech thee to grant that what this day was spoken may not be in vain: & that you will please to accept of my weak endeavours O my Lord remember me for good.

27.

Several Irishmen have been hanged in the Castle of Dublin & in many other places within our Quarters of late for robbing & murthering the English. O Lord put a stop to Bloodshed both here & throughout Europe, that at length wee may serve thee with quietness.

31.

I wrote to Mr Leak, Mr Huson, my Bror & Mrs G[uise] this month being ended O Lord pardon the Sins that I have committed in it & enable me to spend the next more to thy Glory.

April 12.

News came that Mons was taken by the King of France. o Lord preserve us & all thine from the power of that Monster Lewis 14 the Tyrant of France, put a hook in the nostrills of that Leviathan, that he may no longer Disturb Europe nor occasion the Effusion of more Christian blood & O Lord pardon him for the blood he hath already spilt & for the many families towns & Countries that he hath ruined, only to maintain an ambitious humour & to carry on an ambitious design, but Oh Lord frustrate all his designs & bring his purposes to nought. let him see that there is a God who ruleth in Heaven & disposeth of the Kingdoms of men. Amen, so be it Halleluyah.

14.

I wrote to the Bp of St Asaph & to his secretary Mr Evans and to Dean Dalton.

25.

I gave Comission to Mr Godfrey to look after my Concerns at Cashell.

My time for many days have been in hard study, especially in Knotty Algebra to divert melancholy thoughts these sad calamitous times wherein I am forced to live from home; & do hear almost every day of the murther of some or other Protestant, yet my heart & hope is always steadfastly fixed on the Lord my God & I trust it shall never be moved. I am thine O Lord save me for thy mercies sake.[38]

26.

Lord forgive me for being engaged this day in a study not suitable to the occasion.

May 10.

How have I fallen from my first Love! have there been no remarkable occurrences between my God & me all this while? I have this day renewed my Covenant with thee O my God, grant that I may renew my communion with thee, O Lord. Grant me to understand in Spiritual understanding & my Soul shall live[39] but thy name be glorified, whether in my salvation or destruction. I give up my Soul, my Life, my all, wholly to thee, from whom I rece^d them to be disposed of as may make most for thy Glory & thy will be done. Oh let it be done.

14.

I wrote to the Bp of St Asaph concerning Bp Gore of Waterfords will of which I sent him a copy.

17.

The actions of my life are inconsiderable; thou O Lord knowest the breathings of my heart accept them I beseech thee pardoning my failures of the days past & graciously receive my thanks for the mercies of them.

18.

Thy name be praised O Lord for all thy mercies, this Evening I invented a way to find out the Moons distance from the Center of the Earth without the help of its Parallaxe.

28.

I wrote to my Bro^{r} & to Mrs Guise.

31.

This Day I had holy Communion with the Lord, Oh my God give me many more such & that my Soul may be edifyed thereby.

June 7.

God's Holy Name be for ever praised for this days heavenly communion with him. O grant me many more such & my Soul shall live for ever.

11.

I wrote to the ABp of Canterbury to Mr Brocas & to Dr Pocock.

I am thine O Lord forsake me not utterly.

21.

I have for many days gone on in the ordinary tract, without any thing remarkable, but this Day I had holy Communion with God. Oh grant me many such & my soul shall live & gracious Lord give me strength to perform my Vows, for without thee I can do nothing.

23.

To Dean Pullein & Mr Moor of Athy & Mrs Bury I wrote.

July 3.

Was a day of publick Fasting & holy communion with God.

4.

This day by the Assistance of God (whose name be for ever glorifyed) I presently found out an answer to this Question.

[*three-quarters of page blank*].

26.

Mr Willm Fitzgerald Dean of Cloine was consecrated Bp of Clonfert in Christchurch in Dublin, by Francis Lord ABp of Dublin, Anty Ld Bp of Meath, Willm Ld Bp of Kildare & W Ld Bp of Rapho assisting in which consecration I had no hand (God's name be praised for it) nor may I ever be concerned in bringing unworthy men into the Church.[40]

Aug 9.

This day I consecrated Dr Nath: ffoy Bp of Waterford & Lismore in St Bridgets Church in Dublin Anth Ld Bp of Meath [*blank*] Ld Bp of Killalow & Willm Ld Bp of Raphoe assisting. O Lord make him an Instrument for thy great glory, as I have great hopes that he will be, let the work prosper in his hand,[41] & O Remember me for good.

18.

I wrote to the ABp of Canterbury Dr Bury & his wife, Mrs Guise & Mr Leigh.

22.

I wrote to Mr Ash at Vienna & to my Lady Carey.

Sept 3.

I recd a letter from Mr Justellus & another from the Bp of Salisbury. I have followed my studies well I thank God for sometime past but nothing remarkable has occurred to me; & that it hath not O Lord pardon me & make my studies, thoughts & desires all to tend to thy Glory, & above all things fit & enable me to do thee service in the station wherein thou hast set me, that I may seek thee only.

20.

We have consulted some days About preparing Acts agt the next Session of Parliamt & since My Lord Primate Boyle would not hearken to the abridging the power of granting faculties, or rather to a more moderate use of it, than hath been practised we have drawn up a Letter to my Lord ABp of Canterbury (done by Fra: Ld ABp of Dublin to get the power limited & some other things regulated wch letter is Signed by Fr:

Dublin, Narcis: Cassel; Ant: Midens; Will: Derrens; Nat: Waterford. The rest of the Bps here, Viz^{t} Willm: Darens; [*blank*] Aladens; Willm: Clonfert not being favourable thereunto O Lord bless our good intentions & endeavours for the benefits of the Church.[42]

Octo^{r}: 8.

I sent a Copy of a Letter signed by the Archbp of Dublin, myself, the Bps of Meath, Derry & Waterford for the Archbp of Canterbury concerning the reformation of abuses in this Church especially concerning (1) faculties for pluralities (2) Examinations for orders & admission into Ecclesiastical livings (3) recovering Ecclesiastical Debts (4) the use of Excommunication this Copy I sent to the Bishop of St Asaph, but since that another copy is ordered, To be drawn & that laid by. O God remember me for good & cause these abuses to be reformed & put it into the heart of those concerned to do it.

Yesterday came the news of Lymerick's surrender[43] wch on how much the worse conditions it be done by so much the better let us endeavour to be, that by our much wanted reformation we may prevail with God to be gratious to us. Spare us good Lord & bring not thy heritage in this Kingdom to confusion, we beseech thee, tho our sins have deserved it & the times threaten it & 'tis to be feared that 'twill be the effect of the unhappy conditions that (I know not how or why) have been granted to a rebelious people that were not able to defend themselves, but will in a very little time again offend & go near to destroy us. O Lord be mercifull & prevent what otherwise we cannot escape.

This day came the news of the french fleet's being come into the Bay of Bantry, others say they are on the Coast of Dingle I Couch; but most do think tis only a blind to make people swallow the Articles of Limerick the easier. (But since this time we are assured the french fleet is come in though not when reported)[44]

The Letter before mentioned as designed to be sent to the ABp of Canterbury was laid by & another obtained from the Lords Justices (Sr Charles Porter & Mr Coningsby) to my Lord Sidney (one of the principal Secretaries of State in England) desiring him to represent the thing to his Majesty & to obtain his Letter to the Primate, requiring him to call together the Bps here present to consider of a way to rectify these abuses.

Nov 1.

Nothing remarkable hath occurred to me in many days. O Lord pardon the Coldness of my heart & negligence in my study. I desire nothing but thee, O make me thine, I most humbly beseech Thee.

2.

This Day I wrote to the ABp of Canterbury & the Bp of London in behalf of M^{r} McNeal Dean of Down.[45]

3.

This day about three of the Clock came General Ginkle into Dublin, who was met about 2 miles out of town by the Lords Justices incognito (into whose Coach he went & rode for some time, till the Justices strook off, when he got on horseback & so rode into town) he was met at the same place (called Fox & Geese) by all persons of Quality then in town in their Coaches & conducted to the town where he was received by all the Militia of Dublin (being 600 in number) that were disposed on each side the Streets &c.

Dec. 4.

I came from Dublin to Stapletown[46] through many dangers. The Lord make me thankfull for his great deliverances. Amen. Amen.

Jan. 4 [1692 n.s.].

I wrote to the Bp of London on Sr John Ivory's acc^{t} for the fort of Duncannon. Since my coming into the Country various business & the being unsettled hath made me neglect this necessary work wch now I intend by the help of God to resume again this 12th of Janry (being now in my 53^{d} year) so help me God.

17.

My heart, O Lord, hath been long dead & praised be thy name that thou beginnest to put life into it again.

23.

I wrote to the ABp of Canterbury & ye Bp of Salisbury on Dr Huntington's Acc^{t} for the Bprick of Kilmore, like to become void by Dr Wm Sheridan[47] (the present Bp thereof) his refusing to take ye new oaths of allegiance & fidelity to K: W^{m} & Q. Mary. O Lord if the thing succeeds make it tend to thy Glory, & me to be an Instrument thereof, than wch my Soul thirstest after nothing more ardently. **γενοιτο, γενοιτο** [let it happen].

The way of finding & expressing any number of middle proportions betwixt any two numbers given which was mentioned Jan: 6. 1690/1 I now expressed by the two following tables.

[*four and a half pages blank*]

May 8.

Tho I have been long wandering in my thoughts & busied about many things yet God hath at length been pleased to bring them back again unto himself. O Lord Fix them there, let them rest & dwell upon thee for ever; let me for ever be taken up with the Contemplation of thine infinite perfections, & for ever enjoy the sweet influences of thy holy spirit **γενοιτο, γενοιτο** [let it happen] Sweet Jesus for I am thine & would have none else besides thee.

15.

This day I preached at Staplestown on Eph. 2.8 & 9 & administered the Sacram^{t} to the great comfort of mine own soul & I hope to that of others. God's name be praised.

24.

This day I wrote to Serj^{t} Alan Broderick concerning lands in the Diocese of Cashell (formerly belonging to Mrs Allen that was married to my Ld Lisburn) wch for want of heirs are to be bestowed on pious uses. The Lord prosper the design that whatever comes from thee may return back again to thee by redounding to thy Glory.

28.

This day came the news of thy wonderfull providence, O God, in giving us Victory over the french fleett. Make us thankfull we beseech thee for this thy mercy & great deliverance & let us shew it forth in a holy life & conversation.

June 8.

This Day I rec^{d} a particular account in print of every days action from May the 18th when the Engagem^{t} at Sea began untill May 25 Inclusive,[48] all wch time our fleet were fighting pursuing & burning the french fleet, in which time were destroyed about 23 of their men of warr & 20 of their Transport ships that are mentioned; how many more is not yet known. Lord make us thankful for so great a Victory & thereby for our Deliverance from French Tyranny.

July 8.

The certain news of the French King's having taken Namur (the Castle I mean the town being taken some days before) by Surrender, in sight of the Confederates Army & also of the Emperor's forces under General Housler having taken Great Maradin likewise by Capitulation on June 5th, Stylo novo, came this day. God make us thankfull for this last good & bear the other with patience & Christian resolution & to say Thy will be done.

18.

I came from Stapleton to Feathard & God be praised had a good Journey.

24.

I preached at Feathard on Psalm 16.8.

27.

This day I had my Primary Visitation at Cashell where I gave a strict charge to the Clergy for reformation of what was amiss, wch I pray God they may observe.[49] I designedly erred in nothing, yet I beseech thee O God to forgive me my unwilling Errors & Imperfections.

28.

This day I held my first Court upon an Appeal from Waterford (having continued my Visitation) O Lord grant that both I & my Chancell^{r}, & all others concerned in that Court may allways do Justice, that the innocent may not be oppressed nor ye guilty escape unpunished & ability to do this I beg for me & them for Jesus Christ his sake Amen.

Aug: 11.

I concluded my visitation at Cashell, but first declared Archdeacon Duffy's[50] place & Mr Delany's[51] union of Tipperary to be void.

17.

I preached a Fast Sermon at Feathard on Ezech 18.30.
Lord make it to the salvation of the Souls of all that heard me.

Sept: 26.

I have spent a fortnight & a half in Dublin mostly in idleness & little better than vanity. Lord forgive me what is past & help me to better health that I may amend for the future.

Oct. 5.

The Parliam^{t} met at the Parliam^{t} house in Dublin, all the Bps & Temporal Lords in their parliamentary robes, who being sate My Lord Visc^{t} Sidney, then Lord Lieutenant of Ireland, entered in Royal robes, who (being seated on the Throne & the house of Commons called to the bar of the Lords house) read a very kind Speech, the design of wch was for so much money to be raised as would satisfy to defray the charges of the nation.[52]

9.

I preached at both houses at Christ Church, my Lord Lieuten^{t} not being there by reason of his Indisposition that had kept him from coming to the House on Friday to approve of the Speaker of the house of Commons who is Mr Levias[53] the Sollicitor General.

10.

My L^{d} L^{t} came to the House & approved of the Speaker after he had withdrawn wee settled the 5 Grand Committees, & one other to Inspect former Journals & give an acc^{t} of what former rules had been made for the house. I was chosen of the Comittees for religion & grievances. The Lord enable me to discharge my duty therein to his honour & Glory.

12.

We passed a bill of recognition of their Majestys Title to the Crown & sent it down to the house of Comons.

After the 3^{d} reading & passing the manner was, that my Ld Chancell^{r} taking the bill into his hand (as it was engrossed) asked the consent of the house what should be the title of it, & this was agreed upon to be the method of the house & a rule for passing of bills.

We drew up heads of a bill for abolishing popish holidays at the Committee of religion.

13.

The bill of recognition passed the house of Commons without any alteration & was brought up to the house of Lords by Mr Boyle, eldest Son to my Lord Clifford & Grandson to the Earl of Cork, he making 3 Obeysances, my Lord Chancellor wth some of the Lords (4 are enough) going down uncovered to the L^{ds} bar & receiving the bill wch he delivered without any more than that they had returned the bill entitled &c without any alteration. A Committee for inspecting what acts of Parliament in Ireland that are Expired or do cease with this Session be fit to be renewed was appointed the Judges having before made a report of five acts, that are expired, viz 14 Car 2^{d} Cap. 10. Cap. 13, 17 & 18 Car: 2^{d} Cap. 11. 12. 13.

14.

A Committee for inspecting what acts in force in England & not here may be fit to be passed in this Kingdom, was appointed at the motion of my Lord Barrimore. I was chosen Chairman of the Committee for temporary acts appointed yesterday. This day the house was called over.

15.

This day 'twas voted in the Committee for religion that a bill for toleration be desired with this Provisoe, that the Sacramental test be imposed as it is in England; & also that persons obliged to take it do likewise receive the Communion thrice in the year at least according to the Rubrick of the Communion service & also that they presume not to preach against our Church in their meetings under the penalty of £100 the first time £200 second time & losing the benefit of the toleration for the 3^{d} offence wth some Other Clauses.[54]

My L^{d} L^{t} at a Committee of the Councill promised to return the bill for Toleration that had been drawn without the above mentioned limitations & to get it amended in England.

17.

This day the house was called over.

18.

The whole house of Lords waited on my L^{d} L^{t} with an address to desire his Excellency to interceed with their Majestys that a competent number of men of war may be ordered to the harbours of Ireland to secure the Irish coasts from French privateers.

19.

At a Committee of religion several heads were discoursed on (& by the members of the committee agreed on) as fit to be inserted in a bill for toleration; but my Lord Coningsby's acquainting the Committee that a bill for that purpose was already sent over to England by the Councill, they were let fall.

20.

This morning the house of Lords was resolved into a Grand Committee of the whole house to consider what was to be done with the defaulting members that did not appear at the house upon the Summons, & 'twas resolved upon the point concerning the popish Lords that the Speaker should write to them to summon them a second time & if those in England do not attend the house by ye 21 of Nov. & those in Ireland by the 27th of Octo^{r}, they shall be fined as followeth Viz^{t} Every Earl £150. Every Viscount £100. & Every Baron £100 Marks.

This Evening I wrote to the Bp of Coventry & Litchfield concerning the bill for toleration to be transmitted out of England.

21.

The house again resolved into a Committee of the whole house to finish the business of the last day concerning the defaulters who are Protestants & 'twas resolved that all who are members of the Parliam^{t} in England (wch is to sit Novr 4) be excused from their attendance here; as also that all L^{ds} (popish & protestant) who are in the King's Service be excused by ye house as outlawd & Minors are excused of Course.

23.

The Bp of Cork preached boldly against the Irish.

24.

The thanks of the house were voted to be given to the Bp of Cork for his Sermon wth their desire that he would print it;[55] & this message to be carried to him by the Earl of Droghada & the Viscount Blessington. The ABp of Tuam made a *motion* <Mem: that this motion was made on the 22 day being Saturday> that an address of thanks should be made to his Majesty for his great care of Ireland in venturing his person for its reduction &c. & that thanks should be given to both houses of Parliam^{t} in England for their assistance therein in a Parliamentary way; & thanks also be given to the people of England for their Charity towards the English that fled out of Ireland thither for their security all wch was voted & a Committee chosen to draw up an address to the King, & to consider how the two latter were to be done.

25.

The Committee brought in the address wch was read & after some few alterations approved & 'twas concluded that the Speaker should write to the Speaker of both houses in England to signify the thanks of the Lords house & that in his letter to the Speaker of the house of

Commons he should insert a clause to testify the thankfulness of the people of this Kingdom for their relief in England.

26.

The Address being ready, was sent to the house of Commons for their concurrence, who after some time returned it without any alteration; & that they would attend with a Committee of their house to present it to my L^{d} L^{t}, thereupon the house of Lords chose a Committee consisting of eight, being two of each bench & acquainted the Commons therewith, who appointed double the number of their members to attend the delivery of the address to my L^{d} L^{t} — three bills were brought into the house this day & read the first time Viz. 1. for encouraging protestant Strangers. 2. for punishing Soldiers. 3. to prevent suits for any Miscarriages that may have been committed by such as assisted the King in the reduction of Ireland.

The Committee of grievances moved to have witnesses sworn at the Bar upon complaint of exacting fees.

27.

The Bills were read a second time & ordered to be engrossed. A motion was made from the Committee of Religion that they might have liberty to prepare heads of a bill for toleration, of another bill against Sabbath breakers & for reforming the lives of the Laiety & Clergy which passed & also the house agreed with their Committee that the Popish Holidays ought to be abrogated; but there was no vote passed for preparing heads of a bill for that purpose. At 4 in the afternoon the Address was presented to the Lord Lieutenant.

28.

The bills were read a 3^{d} time, passed the house & were sent down to the Commons. The Committee for grievances ordered all tables for fees belonging to the Civil & Spiritual Courts to be brought into them & likewise a List of ye fees belonging to all offices in passing all patents together with the fees of Honour. Lord be merciful to me a Sinner & enable me to be serviceable to thy Glory.

24.

My L^d L^t by the Queen's orders, commanded me, the Bps of Meath, Kildare, Rapho, Clogher & Waterford to give him our opinion sincerely whether we thought Dean Synge qualifyed for a Bishop.

25.

We gave our Joint opinion in writing that being a man of an ill fame, we could not Judge him qualifyed for a Bp unless he did purge & clear himself of that fame.[56]

I gave an acc^t hereof to the Bps of London, Coventry & Salisbury.

Lord preserve me in this hazardous undertaking I beseech Thee.

29.

This day was brought up to the house of Lords from the Commons by Coll. Smith a bill for increasing the excise, Viz^t to lay 1^s. 6^d additional excise on ale & beer at above 6^s per barrel; 6^d on beer under 6^s per barrel; 3^d on every Gallon of brandy &c: & 7^d on every Gallon of Balcon; which bill was read three times this morning & passed.

31.

The Earl of Cavan preferred a Petition against his Uncle Lambart who is a member of the Commons house; which was referred to a Committee.

Nov: 1.

The Committee reported that the Pett^n should be laid by & that the house of Commons should be acquainted that Mr Lambart pleaded privilege in a business of trust; which is not allowed in the house of Commons in England.

This afternoon the Archbishop of Dublin acquainted us (the 6 Bps before mentioned) that he had received an order from my L^d L^t upon Dean Syng's Petition that he & the Dean & Chapter of St Patricks should enquire into the matter of the ill fame of Dr Synge; but not having authority thereby to summon & swear witnesses his Grace thought that he could not act thereby.

We also passed in the Committee of religion heads of a bill for abrogating Popish Holidays.

3.

Dean Synge put in a Petition, that he might be purged of an ill fame (that was objected ag^{t} him) at the L^{ds} Bar. The Pet^{n} was admitted, but the ABp of Cashell, Bps of Meath, Derry & Waterford dissented. Then the house in a confused tumultuous manner desired the Speaker to acquaint his Excellency the L^{d} L^{t} that they made it their request the Queen would take no notice of any private whispers concerning Dean Synge untill he had purged himself at the bar of the Lords house.

My L^{d} L^{t} thereupon imediately entered the house in his Royal robes & the house of Commons being come in passed three acts 1. of recognition. 2. for an additional Excise 3. for encouraging strangers to plant in this Kingdom. & then in a Speech checked the house of Commons for laying by a bill that was prepared for laying a Tax on Corn; & for voting thereupon that all money bills ought to have their rise from them; & likewise for laying by a bill for punishing of Soldiers. then his Excellency entered in a protestation ag^{t} their proceedings in his Majesty's name to maintain the prerogative & then prorogued the Parl^{t} untill April 6 next following.

O Lord look upon me in mercy, & deliver me from the great calamities & troubles that this affair is like to bring upon me, wherein I endeavour only to discharge good Conscience, Oh Lord, & that Thou knowest, who knowest all things, Hear me O God, hear me & deliver me I most humbly beseech Thee.

9.

We the Bps concerned agreed upon a Letter to be sent to my L^{d} ABp of Canterbury representing the whole of Dr Syng's business to his Grace wch was Subscribed by all the 6 Bps But Kildare & Rapho. The 4 Subscribers also sent letters to their friends to the same purpose Viz^{t} —I to the Bp of Coventry & L. the Bp of Meath to the Bp of London. the Bp of Clogher to the Bp of Lincoln & the Bp of Waterford to the Bp of Salisbury; & the Bp of Derry also wrote to the Bp of Worcester. L^{d}

grant these Letters may have their due effect to the Glory of thy name & the good of thy Church.

24.

About this time I rec[d] a letter from the Bp of London about this affair which I answered by the next post, being then at Stapleton.

1692/3 [o.s./n.s.]

Jan. 5. Nothing remarkable hath occurred to me all this time for w[ch] I beg thy forgiveness, O my Saviour & thanks be to thy holy name that I have begun this Year in health; may I continue so if it be thy good pleasure yet not mine but thy will be done. the fear of the french's landing here doth still alarm us. O Lord put a hook in the Mouth of that Leviathan in thine own time[57] **γενοιτο, γενοιτο** [let it happen].

March 5.

I have spent all this time in my studies at Stapleton near Carlow & in contemplating thy wonderful works & thy gracious dealing towards me O thou God of my salvation, enable me by thy grace to live answerable to thy mercies I most humbly beseech thee.

9.

I came to Fethard.

18.

I held my visitation at Cashell wherein I ordered many things (by the wonderful favour of thee my God) for the good of my Diocese.

19.

On Sunday I preached in S[t] John's Church & confirmed in the forenoone & afternoon to the number of 75 persons; Thy holy name be praised, O Lord for these & all other thy mercies.

26.

I preached at Fethard & confirmed 27 persons. Glory be to God.

1693 [o.s./n.s.]

April 26.

This evening at six of the Clock, we met at the Provost's Lodgings in Trinity Coll. Dublin, in order to the renewal of our Philosophical meeting, where Sr Richard Cox[58] (one of the Justices of the King's bench) read a Geographical description of the *City & County of Derry* & of the County of *Antrim*, being part of an entire *Geographical description* of the whole *Kingdom of Ireland,* that is designed to be perfected by him wherein also will be contained a *natural History* of Ireland, containing the most remarkable things therein to be found, that are the products of nature, upon his reading this Essay he was admitted fellow of this Society together with Dr John Vesey Ld ABp of Tuam, Francis Robarts Esq young son to the Earl of Radnor, some time Ld Lt of Ireland.[59] O Lord grant that in studying thy works we may also study to promote thy Glory (wch is the true end of all our studies) & prosper O Lord our understanding for thy name's sake.

May 3.

Mr Robarts brought in at our meeting a paper of seeming Paradoxes that I have here inserted.[60]

7.

I recd the Communion in Christchurch Dublin. Ld make me mindfull of the renewal of my vows & strengthen me with thy grace to perform them unto my Life's End. Amen. Amen.

11.

I found out the solution of these 4 propositions.

[*two pages blank*]

May 25, 1693.

This day Mr Williams Minister of new Ross in the County of Wexford & Archdeacon of Cashell died of a violent fever.[61] O Lord preserve thy servant who putteth his trust in thee, & at this time lies under some Indisposition of body. Glorify thy holy name by him or upon him.

June 11.

This Day I consecrated Mr Henry Rider Bp of Killalow in the Church of St Peter & St Paul at Dunboyn in the diocese of Meath (leave being first had from my Ld Primate & the Bp of Meath) where assisted William Floyd[62] Ld Bp of Killalla & Nath: Wilson Ld Bp of Limerick.

July 22.

I am by the mercy of God now restored (I hope) to my perfect health after various languishings; for which God's holy name be praised for ever & ever; & grant O Gracious Father, that I may spend the strenth thou hast been pleased to give me to thy honour & glory & the Salvation of Souls. Amen.

1693/4 [o.s./n.s.]

Jan 1.

It is long that I have neither done or received any thing remarkable but the Mercy of God in restoring me to my health is greatly to be praised & to be had in perpetual remembrance by me; grant it may be so, O God, I beseech Thee & that as now I begin the year with a gratefull acknowledgment & commemoration of thy mercies, so I may continue & End it in glorifying thee O God my Saviour Blessed be thy name for ever & ever. Amen. Amen.

[*half page left blank*]

1694 [n.s.]

March 18, I Visited my diocese of Cashell in St John's Cashell.

April 18.

I held my triennial visitation at Cork.

20.

The News came to Cork while I was there, that their Majesties were pleased to declare I should be translated to the See of Dublin & accordingly the King's Letter was sent over for that purpose; & all this without my knowledge or any means used by me for obtaining it O Lord thy ways are wonderful, & as this is thy sole doing, so I beseech thee to grant me sufficient assistance of thy holy Spirit to enable me to perform the work which Thou hast assigned me. Amen. Amen.

This news at first laid me grovelling on the Ground in my Chamber at Cork for the Terror of it.

May 24.
My Patent for the Archbishoprick of Dublin was past.

26.
I was enthroned in St Patrick's in Dublin.

June 4.
I was Sworn before My Lord Chancellor at his house.

8.
I was Sworn of the Privy Councill.

12.
I was Sworn at King's Bench Lord enable me to keep these Oaths.

27.
I held my Primary Visitation at St Patrick's.

28.
I Visited the Chapter of St Patrick's.

July 4.
I visited the Chapter of Christchurch.

17.
I held my Primary Triennial Visitation for the Diocese of Kildare at the Naas.

18.
I held a Parochial Visitation at the Church of Kilcullen Diocese Dublin.

19.

I held my Primary Triennial Visitation for the Diocese of Leighlin & Fernes in the Parish Church of Catherlough [Carlow].

24.

I held the same for the Diocese of Ossory in the Cathedral at Kilkenny.

26.

I visited the Duke of Ormonds free School at Kilkenny.

O Lord grant that all the rules I made in these my visitations may be duly observed & that all may tend to thy honour & Glory.

Sept 9. I visited Athy.

10. *Castledermot*. 11. *Dunlavin*. 12. *Donard*. 13. *Ballymore* in the forenoon & *Blessington* in the afternoon. 14. *Tallough*.

Oct 8.

Bray in the Morning & *Powerscourt* Afternoon. 9. *Rathdrum*. 10. *Arklow*. 11. *Wicklow*.

12.

Newcastle & *Delgenny*.

15. *Leixlip*. 16. *Chappel Izold*. 17. *Manooth*. 18. *Kildrought*. 20. *Castleknock*.

22. *Santry*. 24. *Swords*. 25. *Lusk*. 26. *Balrothery*. 27. *Clenmethan*. 29. *Houth*. 30. *Finglas*.

Nov 8. *Monkstown*. 13. *Rathcool*. 15. *St Brides Dublin*. 22. *St Peters*.

22.

This day died the most Revd John [Tillotson] L^d ABp of Canterbury.

26.

This day I wrote to the Bp of *Leighlin & Fernes* admonishing him not to ordain any, but such as are to be preferred in his own Diocese nor to admit any out of another diocese into his without Letters Dimissory God grant it may have its effect.

29.
I visited St *John's* church in Dublin.

Dec: 6.
I visited S[t] *Michael's* church. 13. S[t] *Nicholas* within the gates.

28.
This morning about one of the Clock died that most excellent Princess Mary Queen of England at her house at Kensinton & left me the greatest of her admirers & faithfullest of her Subjects to lament her Death — & the Loss of the 3 Kingdoms thereby, untill it shall please God to call me to follow her for ever & to be (if it may so please my heavenly Father) where I have good hope to believe she is.

Sit anima mea cum anima Dominae meae hoc est,
in Intimis Paradisi penetralibus.

[May my soul be with the soul of my lady that is, in the innermost reaches of Paradise]

1695

May 30.
I was taken with a bleeding at the nose which lasted by Intervals all that day, & the next it grew more violent, but thro' God's blessing & the care of M[r] Thomson the Surgeon, it was stopt on the third day by pinching my Nostrills close together which I endured for three days & three nights continually, for which God's mercy be for ever praised.

June 11.
This day I consecrated a parcel of Ground to be united to the Church Yard of S[t] James in Dublin, which before was too small.

Aug. 27.
The Parliam[t] of Ireland met & passed on Saturday Sep[r] 7 the following Six Acts.

Sept 9.

The House of Commons voted £16000 & odd money should be raised to pay the arrears due to the army & the Civil List nemine Contradicente [no one dissenting].

10.

This Evening betwixt 8 & 9 of the Clock at night my Niece Grace Marsh[63] (not having the fear of God before her eyes) stole privately out of my house at St Sepulchers, & (as is reported) was that night marryd to Chas Proby Vicar of Castleknock in a Tavern & was bedded there with him — Lord Consider my affliction.

Oct. 12.

This evening a young Gentlewoman (who calls herself by the name of Henderson, & had several times before petitioned me by letters, without any name subscribed thereunto, to send her some relief for her Mother, who had been taken & stripped by a french Privateer coming from England to Cork, where she is now in a miserable poor condition) came to me about a quarter after 9 at night, & staid in discoursing with me alone in the Dining & withdrawing rooms untill after 10, to whom I gave 2 Guineas for the relief of her Mother. I taxed her (saying she was unmarry'd) with being with Child (she visibly appearing to have a great belly) which she endeavour'd to put off by asking me why I thought so & the like, but did not once positively deny it to be so; I pray God to protect & defend me against any evil design there may be in this matter.

Heads of a bill of Toleration were brought into the house of Lords by the Earl of Droghada; but by the Bps voting that they should not be read untill 3 Days after (who had a Majority of votes) they were quite laid by.

The Bps of Derry & Waterford protested agst throwing out of the house a bill for union & division of parishes. & in their protestation having reflected something on the house (as was apprehended) they were both ordered to withdraw & after some time the Bp of Derry was brought in & asked the pardon of the house & was ordered to take his Place, but the Bp of Waterford standing out, was brought to the bar &

there received Sentence to be sent Prisoner to the Castle until he should Submit to beg pardon of the house & desire his Enlargement by petition, which accordingly he did on Tuesday morning and was ordered his place (his Confinem^{t} having been on Saturday).

1696

Augt 17.
The Lord forgive my negligence that I have all this time omitted numbring my days, having spent most of my time in the Country at St Catherines near Dublin.

Sept 8.
This morning the Parliam^{t} met & adjourned untill Sep^{t} 22^{d}.

16.
I returned £220 to Dr Edwd Bernard of Oxford who takes a Journey into Holland friday the 18th on purpose therewith to purchase for my use the choicest of Jacobus Golius his oriental Manuscripts that will be exposed to Sale by auction at Leyden on Octo^{r} 6th next Ensuing.[64]

22.
The Parliam^{t} met & adjourned unto Octo^{r} 1 & thence again unto Octo^{r} 14.

Octo^{r} 10.
This day I answered my L^{d} ABp of Canterburys letter of Septr 19th 1696.

Decr 8.
This day about 4 of the Clock afternoon my Lord Chancell^{r} Porter (one of the Lords Justices of Ireland) fell down dead suddenly in his Chamber having taken Physick some days before for a cold; but after his physick, for two or three Days before this happened he found himself very well, as he said the night before. O Lord teach me to number my days that I may be always ready to run unto thee at a Minutes Call;[65] but O Gracious God & Saviour give me time to trim my Lamp[66] when it

shall please thee to summon me to meet thee, let me know some time beforehand, when I am to appear before my Lord God that I may not do it in a slovenly manner, clothed with the rags of Sin & defiled with the vile corruptions of my nature & enormous practices. But O Lord give me both time & grace to cleanse my Soul from sins, or to obtain thy pardon for them by repentance that she may be presented before thee washed & cleansed by the blood of thy Son Christ & thereby she may be[c]ome spotless & blameless in thy Sight.

O Lord Jesu Christ have mercy upon my Soul for wch thou sheddest thine innocent blood. 'Tis thine, thou hast bought it wth an inestimable price; & therefore to thee I resign it into thine hands I commit it.[67] Lord have mercy on it.

This Morning the State of ye Kingdom of Ireland was brought to me Early by Mr Stone (formerly secretary to my Ld Capel) by order from England; which contrary to my Custom I presently read over laying aside all other business.

Appendices

1

Narcissus Marsh to Thomas Smith, 19 January 1705/6[68]

REV^{D} SIR

I have been the longer in giving you a return to your last, because having been for some months much in the Countrey (tho' not farr from Dublin) I cou'd not so readily speak with the Provost of the Colledge, as otherwise; who sayth y^{t} He never receiv'd any such Letter from my L[ord] Clarendon, as you mention'd to have been sent by Him; which if He had, He would certainly have Answear'd It.

As for Doctor Stillingfleets Books, They are only the printed ones y^{t} I have purchasd and y^{t} for these Reasons.[69]

First, because there are few of the MSs of any note, being most of Them but Transcripts & those relating chiefly to Heraldry and the Families in England & other English Affairs & therefore not so usefull in this Kingdome as there.

Secondly, because the price of the Books altogether was greater y^{n} I could well compas to pay in a reasonable Time; & therefore I was willing to secure ye Printed Books first and that Because

Thirdly there was then a design on foot to procure the purchase of the MSs some other Way, but to be apply'd to the same use with the printed Books, which perhaps may take effect, but if not, then, if Mr Stillingfleet will sell Me such of Them as I shall pitch upon, I may haply deal with Him for y^{m} (if not for the whole) upon reasonable Terms.

In the mean time I have all the Books in my own House in Dublin at the present where I intend to keep Them, until They are perfectly Catalogu'd (which I am now about) and until The Ground & other Things relating to the Government & management of the Library, be settled by Act of Parliament, for which I am now preparing a Bill against our next Session of Parliament.[70] And to put all Things in as sure and usefull a

Method as I can I have procur'd, A Copy of the Rules and Statutes of the Bodleyan Library in order to have something like Them here.

As to what was written to You concerning the College Library I have this to offer. That whilst I was Provost of the College, both the Hall and the Chappell being too little & streight to receive the Number of Schollars, that was then increasing very much every year, I resolv'd upon building a new Hall & Chappell (as well as enlarging the College, to which considerable accessions y^{n} were and since have been made, to the value of above 6000^{li}, nearer 7000^{li}). But I thought it most proper to begin with the House of God, & thereupon caus'd the Foundation of a new Chappell (much larger than the former) to be laid, & before the structure was half finisht, I was remov'd & Dr Huntington (who succeeded me) compleated the work, the College Treasury being at that Time sufficient to pay all the charges. In the mean time the Schollars were forct to attend Prayers in the College Hall. When the Chappell was finishd, the next work was to build a larger Hall; and because the old one could not conveniently be enlarg'd as it stood, it was necessary to pull that down & to build a larger in its Place, both in length and breadth, wch was the work of some Years. Whilst This was doing ye Scholars having no Place to eat in, They were forct to make use of the Library for y^{t} purpose, & because the Books were not chain'd, 'twas necessary that They should remove Them into some other Place, & having no one Roome for Them, They were constrein'd to lay Them in Heaps in some void Rooms.

This is the true Reason why the College Library was rendred utterly uselesse for some Years, but now the Building being finisht (as it has been for a considerable Time) ye Books are again plac'd in the Library and 'tis become as usefull as ever; only I must adde, That whilst the Papists got possession of the College, and Library in the late Calamitous Times, many Good Books both printed and MSs were lost, which cannot be attributed to negligence. I have this further to say, That the Books not being chaind, cannot so easily be secur'd, especially seeing They have no Standing Library Keeper, But one of the Junior Fellows is chosen every year into that Office, for which He only has Six Pounds

Salary. Whereupon when I was Provost of the College, finding the Books by Degrees to be embeazeld, I took this Course, besides the Generall Alphabetical Catalogue, I caus'd Tables to be drawn up & hung at the end of each Classis of the Books (They being dispos'd in Classes) as Yours are in the Cross part of the H in the Bodleyan Library) conteining the Shelvs & ye Numbers and Names of all the Books on every Shelf; ye Books likewise being Number'd or figur'd; & when a new Library Keeper was chosen, I carry'd Him into the Library, examin'd all the Books in his presence, and gave Him a charge of Them, & then at the End of the Year w^n another Library Keeper was chosen, I carry'd both the Old & New Library Keeper up, & run over all the Library, as before (which was not above two Hours work,) & what Books were wanting I made the Old Library Keeper restore or pay for to buy Others of the same kind in their Steed, & gave the New Librarian his charge; and doing this every Year, I kept the Books entirely together, whilst I govern'd that College.

But That which renders that Library almost uselesse to all, but some of ye College is this, That by the College Statutes no Man, besides the Provost and Fellows, is permitted to study there, unless carry'd up thither by one of Them, who is bound to be present all the Time the other Staies in the Library. And 'twas This, & this consideration alone, y^t at first mov'd Me to think of building A Library in some Other Place (y^n in the College) for publick use, where all might have free access, seeing They cannot have it in the College; nor are our Booksellers Shops furnisht any thing tollerably with other Books than new Triffles and Pamphletts, & not well with Them also.

To prevent embeazelling I have provided Chains for all my Books, but the smaller sort, which will be lockt up inter Cancellos, that may be open'd & deliver'd out to be perus'd upon the Place, as Those in the Galleries in the Bodleyan Library are. I have by this time sufficiently tired you on this Subject. I will only add That the Book you mention'd call'd *Systema Bibliothecae Collegii Parisiensis Societatis Jesu* I have neither seen nor heard of before, but do beleive it may be of great use to Me in this design; if I knew how to procure it; & therefore do begg y^t

favour of you to procure it for me; but on no Account to deprive you of Yours.

Now after This long Account of other Matters, I think I cannot act with that candour & Sincerity towards You, that I profess to use in all my Actions, if I do not acquaint You, that lately looking into Dr Huntington's Life written by You,[71] I observ'd (wch I had not done in reading it over before) yt in the 28th Page you Speak as though Dr Huntington and I had procur'd the Old Testament to be translated into Irish, *Illi Interpretem idoneum nacti* are your words. Whereas the Translation thereof had been made at the procuremt of Bp Bidel[72] by Mr Sheridon, Father of Dr Sheridon Bp of Kilmore now in London, before the rebellion in 41 as I have been inform'd; and the whole transaction of preparing it for the Press was after this Manner.

When Mr Robert Boyle had near finisht printing the New Test[ament] in Irish[73] (wch He did by an old printed Copy, done, I think, by Daniel Williams)[74] hearing that Dr Henry Jones, yn Bp of Meath[75] (with whom He corresponded) had then in his Custody the translation of all the old Test[ament] into Irish, made by the pains & procuremt of Bp Bidel (who understood the Irish Tongue very well) takeing to his Assistance Mr Sheridon, a ClergyMan of his Diocese of Kilmore (as I have been inform'd for I had it from the aforesaid Bp Jones) with some others; He desired it might be transcribed & fitted for the Press (because the Handwriting of the Copy was not very fair) promising to pay for the transcribing. This Bp Jones communicated to Dr Sall, ye Convert yn in Dublin[76] & to Me then Provost of the Colledge, & that He was willing to lend his Book for yt purpose, if a fit Transcriber could be gotten, & the Translation & Transcript be examined by Persons sufficiently qualify'd to discover & Amend any Errours in It, Dr Sall imediately procur'd one *Denine*; an Irishman, who could both speak and write Irish very well (which is rare, for very few of all those who speak Irish perfectly well, can either write or read it, wch They are never bred up to, having scarce any Books written in that Language; so that They do not generally knowsomuch as ye Character). But this *Denine* was no Scholar. However Dr Sall employd him to transcribe some Sheets in his own Lodgings at 12^{d} ye sheet, & sent y^{m} to Mr Boyle as a Specimen to see if he lik'd the Writing and price, and sent Him likewise the Number of Pages in the Whole Book, and how many of Them the Specimen took up that so He might be able to compute how much the charge of the whole wou'd amount to at 12^{d} per sheet.

In the mean Time Dr Jones Bp of Meath, being very old, dyed (leaving the original Book in Dr Sall's hands) Dr Dopping[77] Succeeded Him in his Bprick, who was zealous enough for the Work; & Dr Sall being also ancient & infirm, & not able to attend, & wanting help to examine the work, & convenience in his Lodgeings for the Transcriber there to prepare came to Me desireing I would procure a Room in the College for the Transcriber to write for which He was the more Solicitous, because there was at that time, an Irish Priest, a Convert one Mr Paul Higgins in my Hous, and one Mr Mullan, a Master of Arts & good Scholar, bred up in the College (wch I at that Time employed to transcribe *Euthymius's Planoplia* out of an ancient Greek Copy for D^{r} ffell Bp of Oxford) at hand; both able to read & write, as well as speak, Irish very well, who might be assistant in examining ye Transcript with little trouble.

And here give me leave to make a Digression, whereby you may know how I came to have this Mr Paul Higgins in my House. I had not been long in the College of Dublin, after my first coming over, w^{n} Dr Sall (who y^{n} lodg'd in Dr Tho: Price Abp of Cashell's house at Cashell (by whom He had been newly preferred to a good Living in his Diocese) wrote a Letter to Me setting forth, that the said A:Bp had for sometime employ'd one Mr Tiernan, an Irish Convert Priest, to preach in the Cathedral Sundaies in ye afternoon in Irish, to which there was a great concours of people of all sorts that understood Irish, wch He hop'd might conduce very much towards the conversion of the Irish Papists; w^{n} They heard the Truth of the Gospell preacht to Them in its purity, especially if this were practised in many parts of ye Kingdome. This enflam'd Me, & put Me upon contriveing how I might do something considerable that Way towards the carrying on so pious a Work. I presently bethought my self, that by the Statutes of our College, of

Seaventy Scholars of the House (wch is the compleat Number) we were bound to chose thirty of Them *Natives of Ireland*. And tho' by *Natives of Ireland* had been understood, *Such as were born in Ireland*, tho' of English Parents, as well as of Irish; and accordingly They were wont to choos those 30 Natives indifferently of either Nation, provided They were born in Ireland; Yet my opinion then was, & still is, y^{t} the Statute requires those 30 should be of Irish Extraction, intending thereby the better to propagate the Protestant Religion amongst the Irish. I then sent for those Natives, who at that Time, were Scholars of ye Hous, to try how many of Them understood Irish; & tho' most, if not all of them could speak it (as most of the meaner sort (as they generally are) though born of English Parents do learn to speak it, of their Nurses and ffosterers, wch are for ye most pt Irish yet not one of them could either read or write it.) I then took up a Resolution to provide a Man at mine own charges, who should teach Them to read and write the Irish Tongue, & that none thereafter during my Time, should be chosen into a Natives Place, that could not do both, which I observ'd as long as I was Provost. For it fell out very luckily that at that very Time there was one Mr Paul Higgins (the Person abovemention'd) in Dublin, who having been bred up in Spain or Rome (or both, For I do not well remember that particular, but am sure of one of them, according to the information I then had.) was M^{r} of Arts there, & w^{n} He return'd, to his Native country Ireland was made Popish Vicar Generall of Connaught; This Man being brought over to the Protestant Religion by Dr Otway ye y^{n} Bp of Killalla & at that time in Dublin) hearing of my design came and offer'd his Service to Me for that purpose, & I finding Him a reasonable good Scholar, according to their way of education, & having receav'd the Bp of Killalla's testimony concerning his conversation & the truth of his conversion, I agreed with Him for his Diet and Lodging in my Hous, & sixteen pounds per Ann, to teach all the Natives, who were bound to attend Him & as many other Scholars, who had a mind to learn to read & write Irish; & to preach an Irish Sermon once a month in the College Chappel at 3 of the Clock on Sundaies in the after noon. All which He perform'd (& had never fewer than about 300 to hear his Sermons) all the time he stayd which was for some Years until Dr Sall dyed, & then He was promoted by the old Duke of Ormond's Recommendation to his Livings, where he hath continued a firm Protestant ever since, whilst most of Those Natives bred up in the College turn'd papists in King James's Time, & even Mr Mullan himselfe, before mention'd; tho' at that Time a Benefic'd Man in the Diocese of Ossory, & so good a Scholar & so firmly rooted in the Protestant Religion that I thought nothing could, (as he often then protested that nothing shou'd) shake or stagger Him in, much less make Him change his Religion. At First I was much censur'd by some Great Men (& amongst Them by the late Lord Primate, then Ld Chancelor also (as I was told) for undertaking what I have above related, They saying, That Here is an Act of Parliament for abolishing the Irish Language, & I endeavour'd to propagate it, for which I might be question'd by Parliament when ever one should sitt in this Kingdome; but that Discourse soon went off; & I went on with what I had begun).

Thus farre my Digression, where with I beleive that I have sufficiently tyred you I now proceed to what remains in relation to ye *Transcribeing the Irish Bible.*

According to Dr Salls desire I procur'd a Chamber in the College for Mr Denine to write & lodg. About this Time (or somewhat before it, I do not well remember wch), Mr Robert Boyle wrote Letters to Bp Dopping (whom He well knew) to Dr Sall, & to Me, (knowing how farre I was engag'd in the forementioned design) that he had shewn the Copy sent to Him to Mr Reily (a Man very well skill'd in the Irish Tongue, whom He had made use of to correct ye Impression of the New Test[ament] in that Language, & on whose Skill & Judgement, I knew afterwards that He much depended in this matter yt he liked it very well, had computed how much the transcribing ye whole at 12d per sheet, and printing it, would amount to, being about 330li as I remember, that He would pay the 3d part of it (if we could raise the rest,) & that accordingly He had order'd His Steward in Dublin to pay so much Money into my Hands, which He did pursuant to Mr Boyle's orders, whereupon Bp Dopping undertook to raise ye remaining part of the money, & I to get the Book transcrib'd & prepar'd for the Press, in which I us'd this method; When a quantity of Sheets were transcribed, I gott D[r] Sall (if he were able to come of his Chamber, as he seldom was after this,) M[r] Higgins, M[r] Mullan & the Transcriber (& sometimes some other Gentlemen well Skill'd in Irish) to compare the Transcript with the Originall Copy, to find whether They agreed, then to render the Irish into English, whilst I had The Polyglotte Bible before Me to observe whether it came up to the Originall, & where any Doubt did arise (which was very Seldome) after a Debate upon the true Import of the Words, & their Agreem[t] upon a more proper expression, 'twas written in the Margin, & left to M[r] Boyle to advise with M[r] Reily thereupon, but I think very few alterations were made in the Impression.

Whilst we were thus going on Bp Dopping brought word, that He had no prospect of getting any Money for carrying on the Work, He finding every Body averse to it, or else very backwards in it; which M[r] Boyle understanding from Him, desir'd the Work might nevertheless go on, & he would print it at his own charge, as He afterwards did; only M[r] John Fitzgerald, y[n] ArchDeacon of Dublin, & now an Non Juror somewhere in London, sent me twenty pounds towards this good Work, w[ch] I acquainted M[r] Boyle with, and accounted to Him for it; For which great charity of his & many other acts of kindness done I desire, that if you know Him or ever chance to see Him, you will present my hearty Service & thanks to Him.

About or somew[t] before this Time M[r] Boyle had finisht his Impression of the New Test[ament] in Irish & reserving 50 of Them for the High Landers in Scotland (whose Language is perfect Irish) He sent the remaining 450 (having printed but 500 in all) to Me to be distributed amongst the Irish) which I did, reserving (by His permission) 50 for the use of the Natives in y[e] College, lending Them out upon caution given to restore Them upon demand, whereby I kept Them pretty well together for the use of the Succeeding Natives.

All this while I was Provost of the College, and the work went on Successfully (tho' D[r] Sall had been dead some time, & I was thereupon depriv'd of both his & M[r] Higgins help, & had only M[r] Mullan & now and then some other Gentleman also, (& by the by) to help examine &c) It pleas'd God, that before the worke was finisht, I was promoted to the Sees of Leighlin & fferns, for wch I passed my Patent in ffebr: 1682 as I remember, was consecrated on May 6th following, continued Provost till Dr Huntington came over to enter upon the Place in August after or thereabouts & resided in the College until Easter after that, & then in 1684 went to reside on my Bprick, which I had before visitted, & all along taken care of.

In the mean time the work went on with good success, and the more so, because I had now got Dr Huntington's Assistance thereunto; insomuch that before I left the Colledge all the Canonicall Books had been prepar'd & fitted for the Press (being still sent to Mr Boyle, as They were so prepar'd & a fit opportunity offer'd for sending y^m^) & most if not all the Apocrypha, was also transcrib'd, but never compar'd & examin'd. Upon my leaving the College I carry'd the Originall Copy of the Canonicall Books with Me into the Country (there being no more use of it in Dublin, because the whole transcript thereof had been sent to Mr Boyle before that Time) which Book I have still in my Custody,[78] & do now enjoy it as mine own, having purchas'd it of Bp Jones (ye former Bp of Meath) his Executor: But I left the originall of the Apocrypha,[79] together with the Transcript[80] thereof with Dr Huntington, that if Mr Boyle though fit to print it, it may be prepared for ye Press, I having paid for the Transcribing of it out of his Money; But He thought not fit, to put it into the Press. I did afterwards ask Dr Huntington oftentimes for Both, but He protested y^t^ He could not tell what was become of Them. When the Catalogue of the MSs in the College Library in Dublin was printed in ye Great Catalogue of the MSs by Dr Bernard in Oxford, I there found in the Appendix, Bp Bidels Translation of the Bible into Irish, which was no other but that very volume of the Apocrypha, that I left with Dr Huntington, & was I know not how crept into that Library. I sent to search for it, but it is not to be found there, & is, I fear, irreparably lost, by w^t^ means I know not. You mention the Transcript of it wch I left with Dr Huntington, to be now among his Papers, which He going to England a little after the Bible was finisht printing, might know no more wt became of Them, yn he did of ye Originall. Those Papers do really belong to Mr Boyle's Executors, because I paid for Them with his Money; But He left Them with Me, as useless to his purpose, & I left ym with Dr Huntington, & so I fear They will be lost, & with ym the whole Irish Translation of the Apocrypha; unless you can redeem them; which I begg you to doe; or put Me in a way of doing it, which I would do at any Rate.

I have now given You a full & exact Account of all Matters relating to yt Affair, as near as I can; for the length whereof I beg yr pardon. And tho' I have been thus long, yet I must not omitt to return You thanks for your former Letter, wherein You gave Me an Account of many Excellent Authors. I will not now detein you with any Remarks upon particulars; but hasten to Subscribe my Self

Jan. 19. 1705/6 Revd Sr
Your most affectionate Brother &
humble servant
Narcissus Armach:

I hope you'll pardon me for using ye word Dr Huntington all along instead of Bp of Rapho; wch is not done out of disrespect, but because while these Things were transacted, He was only so.

I likewise beg yr pardon for sending this written wth my secretaries hand, because my own copy was so blotted & interlin'd & so long yt I could not well either send yt or transcribe it wth mine own hand.

2

Narcissus Marsh to an unnamed correspondent, 1688[81]

MY LORD
The occurrences of Ireland are So various, yt I shall not presume to recite ym because yr L[ordshi]p recievs ym from better hands; but with one relating particularly my self I cannot forbear to acquaint yr L[ord-

shi]p, because 'twill give some light into ye present complexion of affairs, & discover how Low ye Protestant Interest is Sunk here &c. I was lately cited to appear before my Ld Deputy & Councell upon an information given against me by ye new Soveraign & Burgesses of Old Leighlin, wch is my Episcopall Seat, the whole account whereof here followeth.

The Corporacon of Old Leighlin being an Episcopall Corporacon, erected 500 years ago by ye Bps my Predecessors, Sometime this last Summer there was a Quo Warranto brought against it, but no body ever Serv'd therewith; whereupon Judgmt was presently enter'd up on default, near Six weeks before ever I heard any thing of it. Assoon as I had knowledg thereof I enter'd a Caveat agst ye taking out a new Charter; but wn it was to be pass'd seals, My Ld Chancellor (Sr Alexander ffytton)[82] told my Atturney, yt ye Caveat was put in too late; for his Majesty had now Seis'd on ye Corporacon by ye Judgmt yt was enter'd up agst it; & so I could not be heard upon my Caveat in ye Churches Cause, whereby ye Church has Lost ye Corporacon.

Presently after this ye new Soveraign & 28 Burgesses of yt place (being Irish Papists, very mean men, & living out of ye town; all but one; & not a man of ym yt has a foot of land within ye whole mannor) began to cast about how they might enrich themselves by impoverishing ye Church; & ye way they thought most effectuall was to throw down all ye inclosures, yt had been made (many of them) before ye Rebellion, & thereupon to possess ymselves of my lands, & to make me Plaintiff. And all this was under pretence, yt ye Inclos'd lands originally were Common wch they would lay in Common again, & yt there were Burgess-lands belonging to ye Corporacon wch they would Seis on. The truth of wch later allegation was this, that at ye erecting ye Corporacon my Predecessor gave Church lands to ye Burgesses & their Heirs forever to be held of ye See in ffeef-farm; wch lands being forfeited by ye Rebellion, reverted to ye See again, & were allowed to do so by his late Majestie.

Sometime before ye 4th of September last, ye Soveraign & Burgesses gave out, yt on ye said 4th of Sept: they would throw down all ye Inclosures (as I have Sufficient witness to prove) whereof being inform'd I acquainted ye two next Justices of ye peace (Sr Thomas Butler Bar^{tt} & Mr John Tench) therewith: & w^{n} ye day was come, we all three went to ye town (accompany'd only with our ordinary attendants) y^{t} ye said Justices might record ye riot & committ ye Rioters (if there should be any occasion) & thereby preserv ye peace, & also avoyd ye penalty of ye Statute in y^{t} case provided. W^{n} ye Soveraign & Burgesses were Set forth of ye town in order, we follow'd y^{m} at a distance (accompany'd with some few of my Tenents (whose inclosures were threaten'd to be thrown down) & our ordinary attendants, but without arms, save wch the Justices & one of my Tenents had, wch was no other than usually they bore) & staying on my grounds to observ their motions, w^{n} they (with a Piper before y^{m} & a great rabble of people after y^{m}) came to a mound & attempted to force a way throw it, we rode up gently towards y^{m} & I demanded of ye foremost (one William Cook, a new Convert to their Religion, & a Justice of ye peace lately made) what their design was in riding over my grounds without acquainting me with it (for hitherto they had given me no account So much as of their having a Charter (tho I otherwise knew it) much less of their design) who reply'd, That they knew what they were doing & y^{t} they were not bound to give us an account; one Lieutenant Nash next behind s^{d} that ye grounds were none of mine, for y^{t} I had y^{m} by usurpacion & not by ye Surplice. Upon this they rode on their way, & we withdrew into ye highway at a quarter of a Miles distance to observ their further progress, & w^{n} they came about pretty near us, I rode up by myself to ye Soveraign (leaving my company somewhat behind) & ask'd him as civilly as I could, w^{t} their design was in thus riding over my grounds, who riding on his way answear'd me over his shoulder, saying, we do nothing but by our Charter; and this was all ye Answear y^{t} I could get from him then.

But returning to ye rest of my company, I there found one of ye Burgesses, who said that they were only riding about ye bounds of ye Corporacon, wch said we immediately went home, & left them riding on their way, as long as they pleased; who afterwards made gaps in hedges & rode over severall of my grounds, where they had no right to ride, they being without ye bounds of ye Corporation.

This is a full & impartiall account of ye whole transaction; for wch I & ye two Justices of ye peace y^{n} with me (being Protestants) having been sent forct to appear before ye Councell board, upon a Petition given in agst us by ye s^{d} Soveraign & Burgesses, complaining, That when they were riding ye Liberties of ye Corporacon, I came in pursuit of them in ye head of 50 armed men, & besetting ye way made y^{m} stand, & though they told me their design in coming thither was only to ride ye franchisys, yet with threats & menaces I dispers'd y^{m}, so y^{t} they could not go on with the King's business, nor discharge ye trust reposed in y^{m}.

When on Oct: 30 we had given in our Answear to this untrue charge, according to ye tenore of w^{t} went before; My Ld Chief [Justice] Keating[83] observ'd, yt we deny'd all yt they alleg'd, & yt with great probability, it being unlikely yt I should ride at ye Head of 50 armed men, & use violence to y^{m}, as they Set forth. He farther observ'd, That they had but one witness & to but a part of what was alleged by y^{m}, & he a profligant wretch named Will Reddy who was one of ye Petitioners, whose examinations were taken before Will: Cook, & Nicolas Kelly, two other of ye Petitioners; whereof Nic: Kealy, being Soveraign is Justice of ye Peace only within ye Burrough of Old Leighlin & he took ye examinations out of it. Sr John Davys seconded this; but my Lord Chief Justice Nugent[84] & My Ld Chief Baron Ryce[85] defended ye Examinations to be good. The former of wch two last named pressed it hard agst us, yt we were guilty of a Ryot in riding with 50 armed men (though but three of our company had so much as Sword or pistoll, as we were ready to prove, & ye number not to have been above sixteen persons, & those my own Tenents on my own grounds, together with ye two Justices of ye peace, y^{t} came on purpose to prevent a riot on their side, & to secure me in ye possession of my lands). Hereupon ye Atturney Generall Sr Rich Nagle[86] suggested to My Ld Deputy, y^{t} ye Justices of ye peace ought not to have gone to ye place untill ye riot had been committed, & y^{n} to have view'd & recorded it ffor said his Excellency how did y^{u} know y^{t} they would committ a riot? Whereto 'twas reply'd, yt we were ready to prove, yt ye Soveraign & Burgesses gave out, yt on yt very day they would throw down ye inclosures, wch could not be done by y^{m} without committing a Riot; & y^{t} if they had stay'd untill ye Riot had been committed, I should y^{n} have lost possession of my lands, & moreover 'twould have been impossible for y^{m} to have gotten any to witness agst ye Rioters, because all ye neighbours would have been afraid of y^{m}, if they had succeeded in yt their first attempt. Besides y^{t} ye Justices would have been finable 100^{li} a man, for not endeavouring to keep ye Kings peace upon information given of an intended Riot. When these things had been discoursed (we had again & again offered to prove all yt we said to be true wn they alleg'd in contradiction thereunto) & I expected My Adversaries should at least have been check'd, for putting me & ye two Justices of ye peace to so much trouble & charg, w^{n} they only did their duty, & ye Complainants only were in ye fault; My Ld Deputy y^{n} said yt ye King's charters must not be discouraged; & 'twas propos'd, yt I should join with y^{m} in a Commission of perambulation (wch would be in effect for me to give up ye cause, & to let go at once w^{t} I had hitherto been labouring to hold) & So we were order'd to withdraw from ye Councell board, & left to agree amongt ourselvs & ye Councell in ye meantime let fall ye business.

This, my Lord, is a plain & full (though a tedious) account of w^{t} pass'd on y^{t} occasion; wherein I may easily presume, y^{t} I am ye first example of a Bishop brought before ye Councell board for no crime, & dismiss'd without any Satisfaction. Nor do I believ ye parallell can be found of Sr Tho: Butler & Mr Tench, two Justices of ye peace, who were accus'd as Rioters, for going after a legall manner to prevent a Riot. But we live in an age & Country wherein nothing ought to be esteem'd Strang. I humbly beg y^{r} L[*ordshi*]p's pardon for putting y^{r} L[*ordshi*]p to all this trouble, wch has been occasion'd by my desire to represent ye whole affair simply & sincerely with all its circumstances; whence may be discerned, what favour we are to expect w^{n} such is our Justice. But ye Complainants are Roman Catholics & we ye Defendants are Protestants. I am

My Lord
Y^{r} L[ordshi]p's most faythfull, most humble & most
obedient servant. N[arcissus] ff[erns] & L[eighlin]

3

Extract from William King's Funeral Sermon on Narcissus Marsh, 6 November 1713[87]

I will not pretend to give you a History of his Life, that will deserve more Consideration, than the shortness of time will allow me, and require better information, than I can procure at present. I shall in the mean while content my self with the following particulars relating to him.

XXVII. *First*, I will shew, That he was greatly qualified with all the requisites that make up the description of a good Man, in this *Psalm* [Psalm 112]. And hence in the *Second* Place, that we have reason to assure our selves, that he is entituled to all the rewards here promised by God to such.

The *First* part of the Description of a good Man in this Psalm, is, as I have already observed, a true sense of Religion founded on a right Notion and Belief of the Being and Attributes of God, of his Power, Wisdom, Justice &c. Now none can doubt, that knew the most Reverend Defunct; but he had these at heart, and by all his Actions, and the whole Conduct of his Life, gave the World a demonstration, that he was a true and sincere Christian.

The greatest Enemies of our Faith must confess, That the Religion which our Saviour settled in the World, gives us the most noble Notions of God, the most full and clear representations of the Duties that we owe him, and the strongest motives to obey him.

This is the religion our most Reverend Brother carefully studied, excellently understood and firmly believed. This he cultivated and promoted by all his endeavours.

Our Church has given us a system of that Religion free from Corruption, free from Superstition, and free from all mixture of *Enthusiasm*, of additional *Fancies* or *Inventions of Men*. This he embraced, followed and promoted, and in this he Dyed. If then by the fear of God, we understand *Religion* and the true sense of obligation thereof (and thus it is frequently taken in Scripture) none can doubt, but our most Reverend Brother was highly possessed of this qualification.

Such good Principles must in course produce obedience to the Commands of God, if we allow them a due consideration and attention in the mind. Such a true Faith rooted in the Heart, must of necessity exert itself in holiness, and work by Love: and consequently introduce the *Second Qu[a]lification* that enters into the description of the good Man, which is to *delight greatly in Gods Commandments*.

XXVIII. That our Deceased Father did so, appears *First* from his great *Mortification*, for he allowed himself hardly any other pleasures besides those of his Study, Meditation and Devotion. If a Man love the World or the enjoyments of it, his manner of Life will soon shew it, and it is an easie thing to observe from an ordinary view of the conduct thereof, whether he have any great relish of sensual pleasures, or delights in Riches or Honour; his *Table*, his *Equipage*, his *Discourse* and *Conversation*, will soon discover him. I confess, a Man may for a time play the Hypocrite, and conceal the Genuine sense and bent of his Soul: But it is while he is on some project, to gain which, dissimulation and a pretence to mortification and of indifferency to Worldly pleasures may be subservient; but such a Man can never be uniform to himself; but as soon as the reason of his dissimulation ceases, the Mask falls off, he returns to himself and falls into the course of Life, his secret Judgment approves, and his inclinations lead him to. Nay, even when under the greatest obligation to dissemble, some sudden surprise or inadvertency betrays him, and discover what he is.

But the good Man before us was the same on all occasions and in all stations, Grave, Sober, Mortified, when a private *Clergy-man*, the same when a *Bishop*, when an *Archbishop* and one of the Chief *Governors* in the Kingdom. His advancement in Place, Riches and Honours, made no alteration to his Temper, and what he was obliged to make in his Equipage, was done after such a manner, that it plainly appeared to be unaffected, and that he came into it, rather because his station required it, than because he had any pleasure in such sort of things. So that according to St. *Paul*, he so enjoyed the Riches and Honours of the World, as if he *possessed them not*.

Now it is impossible, but the mind of Man should be some way employed, and take delight in something or other: since therefore the pleasures of Life did not affect him, since he did not set his mind on them, he must have his thoughts engaged on something else; and it was manifest from the whole conduct and manner of his Life, from his Conversation and Studies, that matters of Religion and Heavenly things were most at his Heart, and that he chiefly entertained and pleased himself with Meditations on them.

XXIX. And this appears *secondly*, from the innocency of his Behaviour in all stations, which was so remarkable, that I may say it with confidence, there is not one Stain or Blot to be found in it; allowing for the weakness of humane Nature from which no Man is free: He hath been in this Kingdom about Thirty Eight Years, he has lived in the Eyes of all, in eminent conspicuous Posts, that exposed him to great and many temptations, and obliged many to observe and enquire into his Actions, in all which he lived so, that Malice could not tax him with the suspicion of any one Vice, or any one Act of Immorality. This is a demonstration that Religion had it's full power upon him, and that the Law of God was not only his Study and Meditation, but also his Rule and his Guide.

XXX. The *Third part* of the Blessed Man's description in this Psalm, is Beneficence and Justice to Mankind. So Vers. 4. *He is gracious, and full of compassion and righteous.* That the most Reverend Defunct was eminent in all these Graces, I believe, my whole Auditory will Witness. None was more obedient to his Superiors, nor more indulgent to his Inferiors. It is hard to find an Act of Severity exercised by him in his whole Life, and when obliged by Duty and Conscience to execute Discipline, it was in such a manner, that we may say of him as God says of himself, it *was his strange work*. Isa. 28. 21. It was a force on his Nature, and he seemed to feel the punishment as sensibly as the Person on whom he inflicted it. He had a real compassion for the weakness and infirmities of Men, as well as for their misfortunes, and we may say of him, as Saint *Paul* saith of himself, 2 *Corinth*. 11. 29. *Who is weak, and I* *am not weak? who is offended, and I burn not?* He had a fellow feeling with all in Adversity, and after the example of our Saviour, in all *their afflictions he was afflicted*. He not only considered them with Compassion, but to the utmost of his power assisted them. Witness the multitude of the Distressed he relieved, and the liberal Contributions with which he helped such as were Persecuted for Religion.

Though a strict and rigid Adherer to the Service of our Church, yet so far as I could observe, neither *Dissenters* nor *Roman Catholicks* did ever complain of him: on the contrary they looked on him as a mild and merciful Adversary, that rather chose to Convert than hurt them.

In his Family he was an indulgent Master, beloved of his Servants, and ready to his Power to do good Offices not only to them, but to all Men.

I shall not speak here of his Charity, because that by itself will make a large Chapter in his praises.

XXXI. The *Fourth part* of the Description of the Man the Psalmist reckons *Blessed*, is Prudence in managing his Business, Ver. 5. *He will guide his words or affairs with discretion*. Prudence is the common Bond of all Virtues, by it they are united and consist together. A Man may be very Honest, Sober, Just, Charitable and Devout, and yet if he want Prudence, all these good Qualities will not be of any great use to himself or the World, and therefore Prudence with a little Power and Wealth will go farther to make a Man's self and others easie, than the superabundance of both without it. Now from the following considerations it will appear, that our most Reverend Brother possessed this in a very eminent degree.

XXXII. *First*, he was sensible, that there is not a greater disadvantage to any one then to be accounted a cunning designing and crafty Person: since it makes all Men to be on their guard with him, to watch every step he makes and to cross him on every turn, least his parts and great cunning should over reach them. This therefore he industriously avoided, and chose rather to be wise, then to be accounted so, he did his business very effectually, but with silence and as little noise as he could, by means of his quiet management he was generally in a Calm, tho' in the midst of Parties and Quarrels. He yielded to Time and Necessity, and always behaved himself with great deference and submission to the opinion of his Superiors.

XXXIII. The *Second* instance of his prudence, was in the choice of his Studies, his great application was to Divinity, which was his Profession. But by way of diversion and as an Ornament to his Conversation, he added the knowledge of several Curiosities and Arts, that he found valued and fashionable in the World. Such as *Mathematicks*, *Natural Philosophy* and *Musick*, he did not endeavour to be profound in these; but contented himself with what was useful in them, and with so much as enabled him to Converse and Correspond with those that were the greatest Masters of them.

He found, that the study of Tongues, especially those of the *Oriental*, was much neglected, and therefore applyed himself diligently to them, and was reckoned a great Proficient in them. This kind of knowledge being a thing singular, and at his coming into this Kingdom almost proper to himself, got him great reputation. He therefore applyed himself to it with diligence, and in order to perfect himself in it, and make it the more useful, he purchased a great number of Manuscripts, especially *Arabick*, which are looked on as a valuable Treasure. This recommended him to the Courtship of many great Men, so that you will find him frequently with Honour mentioned in the works of the Learned, both at home and abroad.

We are not competent Judges what he would have performed, if he had thought fit to publish his Meditations in Print, because his great modesty prevented his appearing much in that way, chosing rather to have his Name recorded by other Men in their Works, than by himself, which even in the opinion of *Solomon*, is a great piece of prudence, who tells us *Eccles.* 12. 12. *By these my Son be admonished, of making many Books there is no end, and much Study is a weariness of the flesh*. It is plain, whoever Writes and Publishes Books, creates himself great toil, and is exposed to Contention, Envy and Censure.

XXXIV. But *Thirdly*, the best proof of Prudence is the effect of it, *If thou be wise saith Solomon, Prov.* 9. 12. *thou shalt be wise for thy self*. That is wisdom, if it be truly so, will have an effect on a Man's Fortune and Circumstances, and will certainly advance his happiness. Now this appeared most remarkably in our most Reverend Brother. He came single into this Kingdom, and had in it neither Relation or Acquaintance, and yet without any ill Arts, without Bustle, Solicitation, Flattery or Courtship, he rose from one step to another, 'till there was no higher in the Kingdom, to which he might rise. He was first here Provost of the *College*, then Bishop of *Ferns* and *Leighlin*, then Archbishop of *Cassel*, then of *Dublin*, and then *Primate*: and was in all Changes of Government so far Trusted, that he was Seven times one of the Lords Justices. These are such demonstrations of his Prudence and Wisdom, that you will find few like Examples. Surely he that could do so much for himself, knew how to guide his Affairs with discretion.

I shall say nothing of what he did before he came to this Kingdom, being not fully informed; but by what I understand, he followed the same plain honest methods, he practised here, and recommended himself to the great and good Man Chancellor *Hyde* Earl of *Clarendon*, whose Chaplain he was, and by that made a way to his future Preferments.

Let me further observe, that tho' towards the latter end of his life by Age and Sickness, for some Years he found himself not so ready at business as formerly; yet he had the felicity, as well as prudence, to put his concerns both Spiritual and Temporal into so good hands, that there was no defect in the Management of either. His Diocese being as I understand in very good order, and a great increase added to his Fortune. Which as it is an Argument of his Wisdom, so it is to be remembred for the honour of those that were Employed by him.

XXXV. I come now to the last part of the description of the Psalmist's blessed Man, which is *Charity*. Vers. 5. *A good Man sheweth favour and lendeth*. Vers. 9. *He hath dispersed, he hath given to the poor*. This is the most signal and conspicuous Grace, for which the most Reverend Father Deceased was eminent. On this he seemed principally to have set his Heart, as remembring that our Saviour has made it the chief or only explicite Article, on which we shall be judged at the last Day, and the Mark, whereby the Sheep shall be distinguished from the Goats. *Matt.* 25. 34. *Come ye blessed of my Father, inherit the Kingdom prepared for you from the foundation of the World. For I was an hungred and ye gave me meat:* &c. This was so constantly before his eyes, that his whole struggle and endeavours seem to have been to entitle himself to that blessed reward by the continual practice of this Grace.

XXXVI. To shew how much he excelled this way, I will consider *First*, the *extent of his Charity, Secondly*, the excellent *election* he made of the *Methods* and *Objects* he chose for it.

As to the extent of his Charity, it reached all that were in want, his occasional Objects of munifience were all that needed; the frequent Addresses to him by Petitions and other Applications were so many, that one would wonder he had any thing to spare for other occasions. The *Aged*, the *Decrepit*, the broken *Householder*, the decayed *Gentleman*, found a continual assistance from his Hands. The *Stranger*, the *Convert*, the *Refugee* blessed him for the relief he gave them. These acts of Charity were Privately done without Noise or Ostentation, besides many constant Exhibitions, which were hardly known to any before his Death, such as the relieving Fifty Widows every first *Friday* of the Month, together with many Private Pensions regularly paid the Necessitous.

I reckon among his occasional Charities, his promoting all publick good Works, to all which he was generally a liberal Contributor, such are Churches, Schools, Hospitals, Poor Houses, Printing useful Books, Encouraging Arts, Sciences and new Inventions, for the benefit of Mankind: to all which you will find him one of the first, and most Bountyful Subscribers.

In short, consider all the ways of Charity, wherein either the Souls or Bodies of Men are concerned, and none of them escaped him.

XXXVII. And as his Charity was thus Universal, so in the *Second place*, the Methods he took and the Objects he chose for the principal parts thereof, shew his great Wisdom, as well as goodness.

First, Therefore to enable him to execute his Charitable designs, he chose a single Life, not that he believed, that there was any more Purity or Holiness in Celebacy then in Marriage, there being no ground for such an imagination in the Holy Scriptures or Primitive Antiquity. On the contrary St. *Paul* pronounces Marriage to *be honourable in all, and the bed undefiled*, and advises every Man to have *his own wife*; whereas we have no such Character of a single Life. The highest commendation given to it is, that it is less subject to the cares and distractions of the World, and gives a Man more freedom and opportunity of attending the Duties of Religion, and upon that account may be more convenient for some Men in some circumstances, particularly when there is a probability that some present Distress, Persecution, publick Confusion or Calamity is hanging over us, which will make the care of a Family impracticable or very burthensome. This is all our Saviour says in its favour, *Matth*. 19. or St. *Paul*, in the Seventh Chapter of First *Corinth*. as will appear from consulting the places.

XXXVIII. Suppose therefore, that a Man be quallify'd as our Saviour and St. *Paul* require, that he finds himself able to live chastly without Marriage, and is under no necessity but has power over his own will, that God has placed him in Advantageous Circumstances as to Riches, and those Riches, are his own Acquisition, and lay no obligation on him either to raise or continue a Family; but he is altogether at liberty to give them to whom he pleases. Suppose farther, that such a Person is convinced, that hundreds must starve or live miserably if not relieved in some extraordinary way, that many others must perish eternally without some other means to provide for their Instruction and Education, than their Parents or Friends can afford them; and that applying his Wealth this way may greatly contribute to help and relieve both these sorts of People; but that Marriage will be an obstacle to him, and that if he have a Wife and Family, he cannot so apply his Endeavours or Revenues. Now if on this account such a Man deny himself and choose a single life, he is surely the Person that according to our Saviour makes himself a Eunuch for the Kingdom of Heaven, and he is the Man whom Christ permits to embrace Celebacy. For I take those words, *he that can receive it let him receive it*, to be little more than a permission; but to undertake it as a purer State or more acceptable to God, without any farther prospect of a publick good, is neither agreeable to Scripture or Reason. See Mr *Dodwell's*[88] Discourse on this matter amongst Bishop *Pearson's* Posthumous Works, *Page 182*, &c.

For in general, *Marriage* is the foundation of Society, and in all Common-wealths it has ever been looked on as sacred and whoever despises it, hates his own Species and contemns God's Ordinance for the continuation of Mankind.

In truth, every Man in a Lawful way owes Children to the Publick, except he find, that he can be more useful by restraining himself from the Marriage Bed, and that having Children will be a hindrance to some greater good, that he designs and has in view for Society. It is surely a great thing for the support of a Common-wealth to Beget and Educate Children; but if a Man lay out that for the publick advantage and the benefit of all, which otherwise would have been spent on a few Friends and Descendants; he will deserve not only to be excused but commended.

XXXIX. And as he is commendable that for some great common good denies himself the use of Wedlock, and the comfort of seeing his Posterity. So on the other hand, he that lives single meerly for his ease and conveniency, or that he may be more at liberty to spend on his single self, what is due to a Family, is a *Wretch* and deserves Contempt and Censure: and it is observable, that God doth often give up such to vile *Lusts*, and makes them at last a Prey to some lewed and detestable Harlot.

Of all this the most Reverend Deceased was well apprised, and therefore resolved on a single Life, for this reason only, that he might furnish the publick with some common Conveniencies, that he found were wanting, and for the supplying of which no other Fund was provided beside that of Charity, and accordingly he effectually executed his noble project.

XL. *First*, He considered, that Gratitude obliged him to remember the Place to which he owed his Education, and where he made the first steps of his Advancement in the World, which was at *Exeter* College in *Oxford*. And therefore as a Testimony of the sense he had of that benefit, he contributed about *Thirteen Hundred Pounds* to the uses of that College.

XLI. *Secondly*, He saw that Learning was much hindered in this Kingdom for want of Books, and therefore to supply that defect, and that he might be useful to Scholars, and give them means whereby they might be enabled to discharge their Duties in their several stations, he founded the Publick Library of St. *Sepulchre's*, and the Building of which cost him about *Three Thousand Pounds*. And to furnish it with Books, he bought the noble Collection made by the most Learned Doctor *Stillingfleet*, late Bishop of *Worcester*, which with the Carriage, *Exchange* of Money, and placing them in their Classes cost about *Two Thousand Five Hundred Pounds* more, to settle which firmly for the benefit of Posterity he procured an Act of Parliament to that purpose, for which he had the Thanks Voted him of the whole Legislative Body and Convocation; and that it might not be a Burthen to the Church, by taking away any part of the Revenue thereof to support it, he purchased and settled an Endowment on it, which cost him about *Three Thousand and Five Hundred Pounds*. Besides this, he has left to it all such Printed Books as he had in his private Library, and are not in it already, which will amount to about *Five Hundred Pounds* more, and will make it very compleat in those sorts of Books that were wanting in it before. His *Manuscripts*, that are valued to several *Hundreds* of Pounds, he had promised long ago to *Oxford*, and they are left accordingly by his Will.

XLII. Being a Bishop, he could not but find in his Visitations, that Churches were much wanting in this Kingdom, and that by meanes of *Impropriations* and other Misfortunes attending the Revenues of the Church, there was not a sufficient maintenance for Ministers to serve the Cures, and therefore to supply these defects, he Built or largely contributed to the Building of several Churches, three new ones were lately Consecrated in his Diocese of *Ardmagh*, and to help the Cures, he purchased several parcels of Tythes and gave them to the *Incumbents*. That of *Terfeckan* cost about *Two Hundred Pounds*. The Impropriations of *Drumcar* cost about *Eighteen Hundred Pounds*, with which he had endowed a new *Parish*, and settled about an *Hundred Pounds per Ann*. for serving the *Cure*, he has likewise purchased an Economy to repair his Cathedral of *Ardmagh*.

Instead of providing for a Wife and Family, he has taken care of a great many Widows, that otherwise might have been miserable and a reproach to the Publick, he has Erected at *Drogheda* Eight *Alms Houses* for the Relicts of poor Clergymen and there is further Provision made for the Building and Endowing of Four more, and he has settled for ever Twenty Pounds *per Ann*. for each Widow. The Building and Endowment of which, together with what was laid out for the Economy of *Ardmagh*, cost about *Five Thousand Three Hundred Pounds*.

None can deny that these are great and well chosen instances of Charity, and must contribute to perpetuate his Memory here, and entitle him to a blessed reward in Heaven.

Let me further observe, that besides the Charitable Legacies he left by his Will, he took care to settle in his Life time those I have mentioned; so that he Wisely and Generously made them his own Gift and saw the Money rightly laid out.

XLIII. Nor did he forget his private *Relations* or *Friends*, to whom he left good Legacies, that amount to *Eight* or *Nine* Thousand Pounds, and this he did in such a manner that we may reckon it a work of Prudence, as well as of Justice.

If then besides all his private and occasional Charities, we compute the value of what Remain and are Visible, we shall find them to amount to near Twenty Thousand Pounds. This I observe not only in honour to his Memory, but likewise for the reputation of the Age we live in since by this and several other instances of Charitable Persons it appears, that notwithstanding all the Corruption and Degeneracy of the World, the noble Grace of Charity is not lost out of it.

XLIV. I might upon the whole make many useful remarks tending to his honour and your edification, but I am afraid this Discourse is too long already, and therefore I shall conclude with my hearty prayers, that God would raise up many such Examples, and that many seeing their good works, may be stirred up to glorifie our Father which is in Heaven.

Undoubtedly God's good Spirit prompted and directed him to these good works, therefore let us give God the Glory, and praise him in his

Saints. Let us thank God for making him an instrument of so much good, and not doubt, but this most Reverend Father of our Church, has his Reward with God. Let us celebrate his exemplary Piety and Charity, keep then in remembrance and add our Prayers, That many may be stirred up to imitate him.

4

Jonathan Swift on Narcissus Marsh, undated[89]

A CHARACTER OF PRIMATE MARSH

Marsh has the reputation of most profound and universal learning; this is the general opinion, neither can it be easily disproved. An old rusty iron-chest in a banker's shop, strongly lockt, and wonderful heavy, is full of gold; this is the general opinion, neither can it be disproved, provided the key be lost, and what is in it be wedged so close that it will not by any motion discover the metal by the chinking. Doing good is his pleasure; and as no man consults another in his pleasures, neither does he in this; by his aukwardness and unadvisedness disappointing his own good designs. His high station hath placed him in the way of great employments, which, without the least polishing his native rusticity, have given him a tincture of pride and ambition. But these vices would have passed concealed under his natural simplicity, if he had not endeavoured to hide them by art. His disposition to study is the very same with that of an usurer to hoard up money, or of a vicious young fellow to a wench: nothing but avarice and evil concupiscence, to which his constitution has fortunately given a more innocent turn. He is sordid and suspicious in his domesticks, without love or hatred; which is but reasonable, since he has neither friend nor enemy; without joy or grief; in short, without all passions but fear, to which of all others he hath least temptation, having nothing to get or to lose; no posterity, relation or friend to be solicitous about; and placed by his station above the reach of fortune or envy. He hath found out the secret of preferring men without deserving their thanks; and where he dispenses his favours to persons of merit, they are less obliged to him than to fortune. He is the first of human race, that with great advantages of learning, piety and station ever escaped being a great man. That which relishes best with him, is mixt liquor and mixt company, and he is seldom unprovided with very bad of both. He is so wise to value his own health more than other mens noses, so that the most honourable place at his table is much the worst, especially in summer. It has been affirmed that originally he was not altogether devoid of wit, till it was extruded from his head to make way for other mens thoughts. He will admit a governor, provided he be one who is very officious and diligent, outwardly pious, and one that knows how to manage and make the most of his fear. No man will be either glad or sorry at his death, except his successor.

Abbreviations

Bodl.	Bodleian Library, Oxford
Cal. S.P. Dom	*Calendar of State Papers, Domestic Series*
HMC	Historical Manuscripts Commission
TCD	Trinity College, Dublin

Notes to Introduction

1 See p. 28 below.

2 King's narrative is printed in C. S. King (ed.), *A Great Archbishop of Dublin: William King, 1650–1729* (London, 1908), pp. 1–42.

3 St John D. Seymour (ed.), *Adventures and Experiences of a Seventeenth-Century Clergyman* (Dublin, 1909).

4 Presbyterian Historical Society, Belfast, Diary of John Cook, f. 1.

5 Public Record Office of Northern Ireland, D/1460/1.

6 Nigel Smith, *Perfection Proclaimed: Language and Literature in English Radical Religion, 1640–60* (Oxford, 1989), pp. 33–43.

7 Paul Delany, *British Autobiography in the Seventeenth Century* (London, 1969), pp. 46–54.

8 Marsh to Bernard, 7 Feb. 1693: Bodl., Smith MS 45, f. 23a; and below p. 49. In the month he began his narrative he borrowed books from his friends in Dublin (TCD, MS 10, f. 1v).

9 David Underdown, *Revel, Riot and Rebellion: Popular Politics and Culture in England, 1603–1660* (Oxford, 1985), pp. 192–5.

10 A. G. Mathews, *Calamy Revised* (Oxford, 1934), p. 151.

11 Nicholas Tyacke (ed.), *The History of the University of Oxford*, iv: *Seventeenth Century Oxford* (Oxford, 1997), pp. 468–9.

12 Anthony Wood, *Athenae Oxonienses* (2 vols, London, 1721), ii, 959.

13 For the various accounts of this enterprise see Pádraig de Brún and Máire Herbert (eds), *Catalogue of Irish Manuscripts in Cambridge Libraries* (Cambridge, 1986), pp. 118–24.

14 Marsh to Smith, 30 Aug. 1698: Bodl., Smith MS 52, f. 69. For his interest in Oxford gossip see Bodl., Ballard MS 8, ff. 11, 13, 14.

15 Marsh to Bernard, 9 Apr. 1681: Bodl., Smith MS 45, f. 27; and p. 23 below.

16 HMC, *Report on the Manuscripts of the Marquis of Ormonde* (new ser., 8 vols, London, 1902–20), vi, 427, 432, 514, 528; and pp. 24 below.

17 *Journal of the Very Rev. Rowland Davies, Dean of Ross*, ed. Richard Caulfield (London, 1857), pp. 5, 14, 17, 26–7.

18 *Cal.S.P. Dom., 1691–2*, p. 48.

19 See p. 52.

20 HMC, *Report on the Manuscripts of the Marquis of Ormonde*, viii, 75; Richard Mant, *History of the Church of Ireland from the Revolution to the Union of the Churches of England and Ireland* (London, 1840), pp. 181, 227.

21 See p. 28. For the context see Raymond Gillespie, *Devoted People: Belief and Religion in Early Modern Ireland* (Manchester, 1997), pp. 134–7.

22 See p. 50.

23 See p. 27, 31, 35.

24 See p. 40 below.

25 For the context see T. C. Barnard, 'Reforming Irish Manners: The Religious Societies in Dublin during the 1690s', *Historical Journal*, xxxv (1992), pp. 805–38.

26 Marsh to Lloyd, 27 Apr. 1696: Lambeth Palace, London, MS 942/96. Marsh introduced similar reforms in Armagh after his appointment there (Marsh to Tenison, 12 Sept 1706: Lambeth Palace, London, MS 929/41, printed in Edward Carpenter, *Thomas Tenison, Archbishop of Canterbury: His Life and Times* (London, 1948), pp. 383–5).

27 Bonnell to Strype, 6 May 1696: TCD, MS 2929, f. 226.

28 Thomas Pollard, *The Necessity and Advantages of Family Prayer in Two Sermons Preached in St Peter's, Dublin* (Dublin, 1696), sig. b1, p. 19; Bodl., Smith MS 52, f. 73; [Narcissus Marsh], *The Church Catechism Explain'd and Prov'd by Apt Texts of Scripture* (Dublin, 1699).

29 Bonnell to Strype, 14 Feb. 1695: TCD, MS 2929, f. 221.

30 Quoted in Mant, *History*, p. 109.

31 Marsh to ——, 6 Jan. 1700: Bodl., Smith MS 52, f. 81.

32 *Cal.S.P. Dom., 1700–2*, pp.195–6.

33 Bonnell to Strype, 4 Jan. 1695: TCD, MS 2929, f. 216.

34 King to Southwell, 29 Apr. 1697: TCD, MS 750/1/65–6.

35 Marsh to ——, Oct. 1697: Bodl., Smith MS 52, f. 63.

36 *Cal.S.P. Dom., 1700–2*, p. 196.

37 See p. 43.

38 Marsh to Tenison, 18 June 1695: Lambeth Palace, London, MS 942/65; Carpenter, *Tenison*, pp. 373–5.

39 Marsh to Tenison, 10 Apr. 1697: Lambeth Palace, London, MS 942/133.

Notes to Narrative

1 An allusion to Psalm 90:12.

2 John Conant (1608–94), distinguished reforming Rector of Exeter College

(1649–62) and Vice-Chancellor of Oxford University. He was of a godly inclination although not a separatist. At the Restoration he was stripped of his university post and left the college shortly after for a parish.

3 Nehemiah 13:31.

4 Matthew Wren (1629–72), secretary to the Earl of Clarendon 1660–67 and subsequently to James, Duke of York, 1667–72. He was one of the first members of the Council of the Royal Society, which may be his connection to Marsh.

5 Seth Ward (1617–89), distinguished mathematician and member of the scholarly body which was the predecessor of the Royal Society. Bishop of Exeter (1662–67), translated to Salisbury in 1667.

6 In 1657 a John or Thomas Vilett purchased part of the church land in the parish and seems to have tried to claim the advowson as a result.

7 An allusion to Psalm 119:110.

8 Edward Hyde, Earl of Clarendon (1609–74), was one of Charles II's closest advisers. Accused of treason and impeached in the parliament of 1667 he fled England, spending the remainder of his life in exile.

9 Bridgeman, a lawyer, was a prominent royalist in the 1640s who rose rapidly in the legal world after the Restoration and in 1667 became Lord Keeper of the Seal, a post which he held to his death in 1674.

10 John Fell (1625–86) was a graduate of Oxford and student of Christ Church, but was deprived of his studentship during the 1650s. He was appointed Dean of Christ Church in 1660. In 1666 he was appointed Vice-Chancellor of the university. He was an important patron of scholars (such as Marsh) and university reformer. He revitalised the university press. He became Bishop of Oxford in 1676.

11 William Beveridge (ed.), *Synodikon sive Pandectae Canonum SS Apostlorum, et Conciliorum ab Ecclesia Graeca Receptorum* (2 vols, Oxford, 1672). Beveridge, a distinguished orientalist of the High Church tradition, composed this work to claim apostolic sanction for traditions which were clearly of later origin. He became Bishop of St Asaph in 1704 and died four years later.

12 For this work and its editions see Mary Pollard, 'The Provost's Logic: An Unrecorded First Issue', *Long Room*, no. 1 (1970), pp. 38–40.

13 Robert Plot, *The Natural History of Oxfordshire* (Oxford, 1677), pp. 289–99 and plate 15. Plot (1640–96) was an antiquarian and secretary to the Royal Society.

14 Michael Ward was born in England but educated at TCD. He became a fellow at nineteen, Professor of Divinity at twenty-seven, and Provost in 1675 at the age of thirty-one. Died as Bishop of Derry in 1681.

15 The word is used here in its seventeenth-century sense of 'idle', 'trivial' or 'foolish'.

16 For Marsh's account of his Trinity years see Appendix 1.

17 Robert Huntington (1637–1701), distinguished orientalistist and fellow of Merton College, Oxford. He spent a great deal of time in the Near East before his appointment as Provost of TCD. He resigned the provostship in 1692 and returned to England, but became Bishop of Raphoe in 1701.

18 For this see K. T. Hoppen, *The Common Scientist in the Seventeenth Century: A Study of the Dublin Philosophical Society* (London, 1970), pp. 23–4.

19 Sands is a copyist's mistake for Sounds. Narcissus Marsh, 'An Introductory Essay on the Doctrine of Sounds', *Philosophical Transactions*, xiv (1684), pp. 472–88. The editor of the *Philosophical Transactions* was Robert Plot, publisher of Marsh's earlier work (see n. 13).

20 The substance of this document must be the events narrated in the letter in Appendix 2.

21 William Sancroft (Archbishop of Canterbury, 1677–91); Thomas Lamplugh (Archbishop of York, 1688–91); Henry Compton (Bishop of London, 1675–1713); William Lloyd (Bishop of St Asaph, 1680–92).

22 Gilbert Burnet (1643–1715), though born in Scotland, became Bishop of Salisbury by virtue of his strong support for William of Orange in the Revolution of 1688, having fled to Holland on the accession of James II. He remained a supporter of William, although he opposed royal policy on the confiscation of Irish land after the Williamite War. He is probably best known for his *History of My Own Time*.

23 Thomas Barlow (Bishop of Lincoln, 1675–91).

24 Jeremiah 9:1.

25 Probably an allusion to Psalm 119:112.

26 Marsh is clearly thinking of the Lord's Prayer in the Book of Common Prayer version.

27 Charles Porter, Irish Lord Chancellor 1690–93, was a strong supporter of the Williamite settlement. There was an attempted impeachment of him in 1693 because it was felt he was not hard enough on Catholics. There was another attempt in 1695 in which Marsh was a witness (HMC, *Report on the Manuscripts of the Marquis of Downshire* (5 vols, London, 1924– 86), i, 575). For conflicts with Marsh see below 8 March 1690/1 and for Porter's death 8 December 1696.

28 Henry Sidney (1641–1704) fought with William at the Boyne and became a Lord Justice and later Lord Lieutenant of Ireland. He was largely responsible for the mismanagement of the 1692 parliament and was recalled to England. Thomas Coningsby (1656–1729) came to Ireland with William, but returned to England after accusations of corruption after the parliament of 1692.

29 The Latin here seems rather corrupt. What is here is an attempt to reconstruct the original reading.

30 Henry Hyde, 2nd Earl of Clarendon (1638–1709), was a supporter of James II.

During the summer of 1690 he had been plotting with Richard Graham, Lord Preston (1648–95), who was in correspondence with James in exile. Clarendon was imprisoned in June 1690. Graham fled from England on 31 December 1690 to the Jacobite court in exile and was found to be carrying a message to James II from Clarendon, who was subsequently confined to the Tower. Graham's estate was confiscated, but he turned informer and was pardoned.

31 William King (1650–1729), who had remained in Dublin during the Jacobite occupation, was promoted to the bishopric of Derry in 1691 and to the see of Dublin in 1703. He was a High Churchman, a regular proponent of church reform and an opponent of Dissent, but in politics he was a Whig and served, with Marsh, as Lord Justice on a number of occasions. He preached Marsh's funeral sermon (Appendix 3). For details of his career see Philip O'Regan, *Archbishop William King of Dublin (1650–1729)* (Dublin, 2000).

32 John Tillotson (1630–94) was ordained probably in 1660 or 1661, after which he became curate to the future Bishop of Down and Connor, Thomas Hackett. He was a preacher of considerable skill and the Duke of Ormond tried to have him appointed as Bishop of Derry or Bishop of Meath in the 1680s because of this. He was also actively involved in establishing more tolerant attitude to Dissenters. In 1689 he was appointed Dean of St Paul's in London, and in 1691 he was nominated as Archbishop of Canterbury but died three years later, his death being noted by Marsh in the diary.

33 Psalm 57:7.

34 Probably an allusion to Jeremiah 16:19 or Psalm 28:7.

35 Matthew 6:10, Luke 11:2.

36 The phrase 'the Holy One of Israel' is most commonly found in the prophecy of Isaiah, but the text is not identifiable. Other phrases in this section also appear in the Psalms, but not in the exact form given here.

37 Richard Leake, Rector of Knockgraffon, Co. Tipperary, 1682–1706, and Rector of Kilfeakle, 1684–6.

38 The phrase appears in Psalm 6:4, Psalm 31:16 and Psalm 119:94.

39 Genesis 12:13.

40 Francis Marsh (Archbishop of Dublin, 1682–93); Anthony Dopping (Bishop of Meath, 1682–97); William Moreton (Bishop of Kildare, 1682–1705); William Smyth (Bishop of Raphoe, 1682–93). Marsh's objection to Fitzgerald is unclear; it may have been Fitzgerald's kinship with Primate Boyle. His fears were well founded, as William King noted after Fitzgerald's death in 1722 that he governed the diocese in a 'wretched manner' (King to Wake, July 1722: TCD, MS 750/7/177–8).

41 As n. 40 with John Roan (Bishop of Killaloe, 1675–92). The final sentence is an allusion to Daniel 8:25.

42 William King (Bishop of Derry, 1691–1703); Nathaniel Foy (Bishop of Waterford and Lismore, 1691–1707); William Lloyd (Bishop of Killala [Aladensis], 1691–1716); William Fitzgerald (Bishop of Clonfert, 1691–1722); see also n. 40. Darensis on this list is Kildare. For these events see O'Regan, *King*, pp. 64–5.

43 This must relate to the signing of the Treaty of Limerick on 3 October 1691 which ended the Jacobite war.

44 This entry confuses two things. The *Dublin Intelligence* for 20 October reported that thirty-three French ships had been seen in Dingle Bay on 7 October, but this proved to be only a rumour. The apparent confirmation of this French fleet recorded by Marsh was the appearance of a French convoy in the Shannon, hoping to relieve Limerick, on 20 October.

45 John McNeal, Dean of Down 1683–1709.

46 About a mile from Carlow town. This was Marsh's usual residence in his diocese. For a seventeenth-century drawing of the house see E. P. Shirley, 'Extracts from the Journal of Thomas Dineley, Esquire', *Journal of the Royal Society of Antiquaries of Ireland* iv, new ser. (1862–63), p. 44.

47 William Sheridan was one of the few Irish non-jurors and was deprived of his see in 1691. He went to England and died in 1711.

48 *An Exact Journal of the Engagement between the English Fleet and the French from May the 18th to the 25th* (London, 1692): a single-sheet broadsheet.

49 *The Charge given by Narcissus, Lord Archbishop of Casshall to his Clergy at his Primary Visitation held in the Parish Church of St John's in Cashell, July 27 1692* (Dublin, 1694).

50 A copyist's mistake for John Dassey, Archdeacon of Cashel 1670–92.

51 A copyist's mistake for Solomon Delane, Vicar of Tipperary.

52 For an overview of this parliament see J. I. McGuire, 'The Irish Parliament of 1692' in Thomas Bartlett and David Hayton (eds), *Penal Era and Golden Age: Essays in Irish History, 1690–1800* (Belfast, 1979), pp. 1–31.

53 A copyist's mistake for Richard Levinge, Solicitor General 1690–95 and 1704–9. From Derbyshire, Levinge came to Ireland in 1690. He was a member of the 1692 parliament and its Speaker. He was replaced both as Speaker and Solicitor General in 1695. For most of the rest of his career he alternated between Ireland and England. He sat in a number of the early eighteenth-century Irish parliaments, but frequently disagreed with the government and was committed briefly to the Tower in 1700 over the Irish forfeitures. He was briefly Attorney General in 1711–14. He died in 1724.

54 For the politics of this episode see O'Regan, *King*, pp. 68–9.

55 Edward Wetenhall, *A Sermon preached Octob. 23, 1692 before his Excellency the Lord Lieutenant and the Lords Spiritual and Temporal and Divers of the Commons in Christ Church, Dublin* (Dublin, 1692).

56 The issues behind the case of Samuel Synge, Dean of Kildare, are unknown; it may have been Synge's litigious nature that caused him to be passed over. William King had a list of Synge's cases among his papers: TCD, MS 1995–2008/37a; see O'Regan, *King*, pp. 67–8.

57 An allusion to Job 41:1.

58 Sir Richard Cox (1650–1733) was born in Bandon and trained as a lawyer. He went to England in 1685, where he became a strong supporter of William III, publishing his history of Ireland there in 1689–90. He returned to Ireland in 1690 as secretary to Sir Robert Southwell, Secretary of State. He was appointed as Second Justice of Common Pleas in 1690, though Marsh seems to think he was a judge of King's Bench, which he was not, although he was frequently a judge of assize in the 1690s. He was a Lord Justice on a number of occasions in the early eighteenth century and became Lord Chancellor in 1703, and Chief Justice of the Queen's Bench in 1711. He acquired a large estate around Dunmanway in Co. Cork.

59 For further descriptions of this occasion see Hoppen, *Common Scientist*, pp. 175–6.

60 Almost certainly Robarts's paper on the mathematics of chance, 'An Arithmetic Paradox concerning the Chances of Lotteries' read to the Dublin Philosophical Society that year; see Hoppen, *Common Scientist*, pp. 121, 181.

61 William Williams, Vicar of New Ross and Old Ross 1684–93 and Treasurer of Ferns 1686–93, married to a one of Marsh's sisters.

62 A copyist's mistake for Lloyd.

63 Daughter of Narcissus's brother Epaphroditus, then living at Fethard. Grace died in 1759.

64 Bernard on his way back to London caught a chill from which he died. It was November 1697 before Marsh's oriental manuscripts, which he described as a 'very noble purchase', arrived in Dublin (Bodl., Smith MS 52, ff. 51, 63, 65). Marsh left them in his will to the Bodleian Library in Oxford, where they now are.

65 Probably an allusion to Psalm 39:5 in the Book of Common Prayer version.

66 Probably an allusion to Matthew 25:7.

67 This is an allusion to Luke 23:46, which is itself a quotation from Psalm 31:5.

68 Bodl., Smith MS 45, ff. 121–5. Thomas Smith (1638–1710) was one of Marsh's frequent correspondents. He was also a manuscript collector and orientalist. As a non-juror after 1690 he acted as librarian to Sir John Cotton, grandson of the Elizabethan antiquarian, in London.

69 Marsh purchased the books of Edward Stillingfleet, Bishop of Worcester, for his library (Muriel McCarthy, *All Graduates and Gentlemen: Marsh's Library* (Dublin, 1980), pp. 38–9).

70 The act was passed in 1707, 6 Anne, c. 19.

71 Thomas Smith, *Admodum Reverendi et Doctissimi Viri D. Roberti Huntington* (London, 1704).

72 William Bedell, Bishop of Kilmore (1629–42). For the translation see Terence McCaughey, *Dr Bedell and Mr King: The Making of the Irish Bible* (Dublin, 2001).

73 For Boyle's New Testament see Nicholas Williams, *I bPrionta i Leabhar: Na Protastúin agus Prós na Gaeilge, 1567–1724* (Dublin, 1986), pp. 72–94.

74 A mistake for William Daniel, Archbishop of Tuam, whose Irish translation of the New Testament was published in 1603.

75 Henry Jones, Bishop of Meath (1661–82), and previously, from 1645, Bishop of Clogher.

76 A. C. Breeze, 'Andrew Sall (†1682), Andrew Sall (†1686) and the Irish Bible', *Éigse*, xxviii (1994–95), pp. 100–2; A. C. Breeze, 'Two Irish Jesuits: Andrew Sall (1612–86) and Andrew Sall (1624–82)', *Éigse*, xxix (1996), pp. 174–8.

77 Anthony Dopping (1643–97) was translated from the see of Kildare to Meath in May 1682, Jones having died in January. He remained in Ireland during the Jacobite period and strongly defended the Protestant interest.

78 Now Marsh's Library, MS Z4. 2. 3 a–b.

79 Now Cambridge University Library, MS Dd. 9. 7.

80 Now Marsh's Library, MS Z4. 2. 4.

81 Marsh's Library, MS Z1. 1. 16 (1). There are a number of versions of this letter sent to various people; for another see Charles McNeill (ed.), *The Tanner Letters* (Dublin, 1943), pp. 494–6.

82 Alexander Fitton was descended from New English colonists of the sixteenth century who also retained property in England. By virtue of this, he was created Baron Gawsworth in 1689. As a supporter of James II he was appointed Lord Chancellor of Ireland in February 1687. He later fled to the Jacobite court at St Germains.

83 John Keating, of the Kildare branch of the family, was Chief Justice of Common Pleas 1679–91 when he committed suicide.

84 Thomas Nugent was a Jacobite who was appointed Chief Justice of King's Bench in 1687. He was restored to his estates under the Treaty of Limerick.

85 Stephen Rice, Jacobite Chief Baron of the Exchequer from 1687. He was restored to his estates under the Treaty of Limerick and died in 1715.

86 Sir Richard Nagle, Jacobite Attorney General 1686–90.

87 William King, Archbishop of Dublin, *The Remembrance of the Righteous in a Sermon preach'd at the Funeral of the Most Reverend Father in God Narcissus, Lord Archbishop of Ardmagh and Primate of All Ireland in St Patrick's Church, Dublin November 6th, 1713* (Dublin, 1714), pp. 24–36.

88 Henry Dodwell was born in Dublin and educated in TCD. In 1666 he was obliged to resign his fellowship because of his refusal to be ordained, feeling he could serve the church better as a layman. He went to London and in 1688 became Camden Professor of History at Oxford, a post he had to resign since he would

not take the required oaths to William and Mary after the Revolution. He died in London in 1711. Dodwell was a prolific author, although which of his works is being referred to here is unclear.

89 *The Works of Jonathan Swift, D.D., Dean of St Patrick's, Dublin* (quarto ed., 6 vols, London, 1755), vi, pt 2, pp. 176–7.

Bibliography

Barnard, T. C., 'Reforming Irish Manners: The Religious Societies in Dublin during the 1690s', *Historical Journal*, xxxv (1992), pp. 805–38

Connolly, Sean, 'Reformers and Highflyers: The Post-Revolution Church' in Alan Ford, James McGuire and Kenneth Milne (eds), *As By Law Established: The Church of Ireland since the Reformation* (Dublin, 1995), pp. 152–65

Gillespie, Raymond, *Devoted People: Belief and Religion in Early Modern Ireland* (Manchester, 1997)

Hoppen, K. T., *The Common Scientist in the Seventeenth Century: A Study of the Dublin Philosophical Society* (London, 1970)

McCarthy, Muriel, *All Graduates and Gentlemen: Marsh's Library* (Dublin, 1980)

O'Regan, Philip, *Archbishop William King of Dublin (1650–1729)* (Dublin, 2000)

Stokes, G. T., *Some Worthies of the Irish Church* (London, 1900)

Index